Two Shrews, LLC
1319 Pond View Circle
De Pere, WI 54115

First Two Shrews trade paperback edition 2019

Two Shrews and design are registered trademarks of Two Shrews, LLC.

For information about special discounts for bulk purchases, please contact Two Shrews Press at twoshrewspress.com.

Manufactured in the United States of America

9 8 7 6 5 4 3 2

First Edition

Library of Congress Control Number: 2019903871

ISBN 978-1-7338890-0-1

ISBN 978-1-7338890-1-8 (ebook)

Cover and book design by Libby Clarke

Art by Nada Kasim

Photography by Kara Counard

The First Winter

Stories of Survival by Experienced Hearts

Bisharo Abdullahi, Nimco Sh. Abdullahi Hassan,
Najma Hussein, Hafsa Husseyn, Maryam Husseyn,
Nada Kasim, Nadifo Kasim, Najma Kasim,
Nasteho Kasim, Nimo Kasim,
Yasmin Nur, and Zamzam Nur

Two Shrews Press
New York | Green Bay

For the women who came before us

Contents

Journey

Family

Faith

School

Plans

Epilogue

The First Winter

Foreword

by Ifrah Mansour

Some stories travel through time, space, and borders. The stories in this book traveled through wars, famines, and refugee camps to bring you a rare spicy slice of the world in the palm of your hands. Brace yourself for an unforgettable ride. From mom sheroes to unbreakable sisterhood, each page takes you on an unexpected journey, propelling you to the next page and to the next author.

How lucky am I to be one of the first readers. I laughed and cried and reached through the pages to grab hold of these generous authors' boldness and bravery. I can feel the sisterhood and the perseverance. I too was once a wide-eyed refugee Somali American girl learning to finally speak my truth in a foreign language.

Beyond these authors' experiences, I am reminded of own shero, my ayeeyo, a farmer and stubborn survivor who taught me to laugh through my pain, to unearth my own medicine, and to keep giving the world a chance to both challenge and surprise me.

Our words might be foreign, our experiences might be alien. But the feeling of longing to belong, the bittersweet sweat of private struggles, and the identity crisis stretching across continents form a beautiful tapestry of humanity. If we listen with our hearts, these stories will connect us, like kindred spirits, beyond borders, beliefs, and politics.

So go on, flip the page: beyond lies a collection of true stories filled with medicine for our divided times, by former youth refugees who lived and thrived to tell their own powerful journeys.

–Ifrah Mansour

Poet and Performance Artist
February 2019, Minneapolis, Minnesota

Foreword

by Bahame Tom Nyanduga

It was a pleasure to be requested to pen a foreword to *The First Winter*. Reading the different articles, poems, and conversations of these brave girls was at times very joyful and at times sad. Their stories about their experiences in refugee camps in Ethiopia and Kenya resonate with me so much, based on my experience as a United Nations Independent Expert on the Human Rights situation in Somalia.

For the last five and a half years I have been dealing with various human rights challenges affecting the millions of people displaced by conflict in Somalia—challenges that the Government of Somalia and its people face as they fight hard to establish a functional state and create conditions for peace and stability. It was the absence of these things, some thirty years ago, which caused the conditions that forced these girls and their families, along with many others, to leave Somalia and come to the United States. They confronted the harsh realities of a nation in conflict and lacking basic services, such as health care facilities, that are necessary to sustain a healthy standard of living. They escaped.

The First Winter tells a tale, or many tales, by Somali girls who find themselves in Green Bay, Wisconsin, in the United States of America. They reminisce about their happy and peaceful lives with their families and friends, remembering family ceremonies and a sense of community before they fled their country. Many write about their different experiences as refugees: One talks of her "big family" of eleven thousand people who knew each other in a camp in Ethiopia, and how she missed them when she left. One remembers the visiting "Carolina's" philanthropy and the joyful Somali song they composed for her. Another girl recalls living under threats of hunger, thirst, and exposure, in spite of all the international humanitarian support designed to alleviate their suffering. "Survival" explains how every refugee hopes that the camps will be home, better and safer than where they came from, though for this author it turned out that every day was a mission to survive. In spite of the sorrow, they survived. These strikingly different stories—

daily realities lived by refugees—will give the reader an understanding, however brief or anecdotal, of the life on the run of asylum seekers.

The realities of asylum seekers and refugees are being lived by many families and individuals (and girls in particular) today in different camps and all over the world. In Somalia currently, there are an estimated 2.6 million internally displaced persons (IDPs), people forced to leave their homes in fear of persecution, whose experiences are not dissimilar to "Survival." Women and girls and young boys are exposed to sexual and gender-based violence in IDP settlements, a problem that has existed since the onset of the conflict, and which continues in spite of efforts to combat it. Refugees are those who escape their own country and cross an international border in search of safety. During an interview at an UNHCR office for resettlement, one of the authors is asked, "Why are you here?" She replies, "Trying to find peace." Everybody in Somalia is still trying to find peace.

It is very refreshing to read in these pages a hope for Somalia. The authors have uprooted from their country, but they have not given up on their culture, their religion, or their aspirations to serve Somalia and humanity. One writes that she wishes that Somalia would have peace, no more wars, no more hatred, and no more enemies. Another says she plans to work with people who are unfortunate as she was, to change people's stereotypes, and calls for embracing diversity of different cultures, backgrounds, and beliefs, acknowledging their uniqueness as Somalis and their common humanity. Some of the girls have been back to Somalia, albeit briefly, and were inspired by the experience to become professionals able to serve their communities in Somalia, in the future.

This book is a must-read for anyone who wants to learn the basic struggles of displaced people and their challenges upon resettlement in any foreign country, particularly Muslims coming to America post September 11th and post Trump immigration policy. In very simple language, *The First Winter* introduces readers to complicated subjects through the experiences of the girls, such as why they wear hijab, and the meaning of Hajj. In one compelling story the author, working at a Walmart, teaches an older American shopper about the meaning of hijab. Also, because American stores don't sell them, the hijab has inspired a business idea: an author describes her plans to sell her hijab and clothing designs to American stores, to make it easier for young Muslim girls to dress themselves without going through the struggles she went through. Another simply notes, "I think some people forget that there is freedom of religion here."

The First Winter tells the story, or many stories, of survival and resilience of Somali refugees, these girls in particular, now in a foreign land so far removed from their country of origin, and what they went through to adapt. Here is the single mother raising children in a foreign land and a foreign culture. Here are the sisters going to school in a new language, in a new community. Here is a letter to their classmates about the challenges of integration. Here is a girl acknowledging how much it meant to her when another student said "hi." At any rate, they are not "invisible," certainly not now. Their stories offer snapshots of family and community life and they express hope for Somalia—and perhaps for America too.

As much as the authors are American, they are very much Somali, by culture and background. Especially coming out at a time when one of their own sits in Congress, one who must have gone through similar experiences, *The First Winter* is an important book. It is short, factual, simple, but very insightful. It will open minds and help American people in Green Bay and beyond better understand Somali people and Muslim people in general. Explaining her experience when she went to Somalia, one of the girls concludes, "In the end I learned to love *my countries*, where I am and where I am from. I miss Somalia, but in Somalia I missed America" (emphasis added).

I commend the authors for putting their stories and experiences on paper. And I commend the book to all.

–Bahame Tom Nyanduga

United Nations Independent Expert on the Human Rights situation in Somalia

March 2019, Dar es Salaam, Tanzania.

Foreword

by Dr. Michelle Langenfeld

The First Winter is a beautifully written collection of stories and poetry by young Somali women, all current or former students of Green Bay Area Public Schools. The young writers came to our schools with limited English and had little knowledge of the holidays celebrated in the United States or how to be part of community that embraces both the "frozen tundra" and the Green Bay Packers. Instead they brought to school firsthand experience and knowledge of dealing with and overcoming much more than most of us can imagine.

Writing about family, love, laughter, pain, religion, homesickness, humility, courage, strength, perseverance and wisdom, the authors take us to a place where it is undeniable that as human beings, we are much more alike than we are different.

I am proud to be part of a public school district that believes that every child deserves to have access to and opportunity for a high quality public education, which prepares students for the future of their choice. I am proud to be part of a community that works to value every member and recognizes and celebrates our differences. And most of all, I am proud to be part of the educational and broader community system that is contributing to the hope, safety, and well-being of the young women who share their stories in these pages.

It is with deepest gratitude that I write this foreword. These stories are powerful beyond measure and inspirational with the capacity to be transformational. They will surely open minds and hearts!

–Michelle Langenfeld, Ed.D.

Superintendent of Schools and Learning
Green Bay Area Public Schools

May 2019, Green Bay, Wisconsin.

Journey

Where I'm From

Nadifo Kasim

I am from Aveeno lotion,

> From thick blankets and cotton pillow.

I am from the house in If Iyo Aakhiro*,

Peaceful, comfortable, and quiet,

> It sounded like birds.

I am from the garden that my aunt planted which looked beautiful in the spring.

I'm from brown eyes and *sambusa* on Ramadan,

> From Grandma, Uncle, and my sweet mom.

> From playing hide and seek and eating dinner
> from one big plate.

I'm from Quran and I believe that Muhammad is our prophet.

I'm from Mogadishu, Somalia,

> From photo albums in mom's closet,

> From the time my sister lost her four
> mandibular incisor teeth when she was four years old

> And they took a couple years to grow in.

I am from the blue flag of Somalia, the same shade used by the United Nations,

> From the five-pointed white Star of Unity.

---

* A zone in the camp. The name means "the light in the afterlife." Nadifo and her family lived near the camp cemetery and passed it every time they went to school.

A Letter to My Former Neighbors in Mogadishu, Somalia

Dear Neighbors,

This is Najma, the girl who used to live three blocks from your house in Mogadishu. There are many things I wish I could tell you. I hope you guys remember me. I hope, too, that every one of you is doing well.

Our house was right next to the Ahlam store. It had a gate wall and was brown with blue doors facing the road. We used to play in the beautiful garden and eat watermelon from the garden when we came home from school. Remember me now? I'm the sister of Ayan, Najib and Mowlid. Remember how we used to gather in our house on Eid days and decorate the gate walls with new curtains and sparkly lights?

I wish I could tell you this in person, but I can't because I'm far away. I went to Ethiopia to complete my sponsorship to the United States. *Alhamdulillah** it went well, and we waited for two years. We were alone there, just me and my three siblings. We couldn't attend school because we were not allowed without proof of our educational backgrounds.

We moved to America on December 1, 2016. Reunited with our family, we rebuilt our memories. I started school again. Life became more meaningful to me.

There are so many things challenging me here, like the weather, the language, and the way I look. It was winter when I arrived and I was like, "What!? I've never seen this thing before!" It was snow. Everyone laughed at me because of the way I said this. English was difficult for me, since I had never spoken with a native speaker before, but I followed along and did well.

---

*   "Praise Allah"

I feel different because of my hijab, but I don't think I should be pushed aside just because people here don't cover their hair. Some of them are curious, and I made friends at school and *masjid*. I have new neighbors, too.

I hope you guys are safe and still together with your families, wherever that may be. Let me know if you will ever go back. When we left Mogadishu there were only a few families left, and the roads were empty.

Do you remember the picture of the four of us? Rahma and Hafsa were standing while Muniira and I were sitting. We were wearing our Eid day outfits. Muniira was smiling. Her smile shone through the picture. We were all wearing the same *abayas* with different scarfs. It is a beautiful picture of a beautiful friendship. Pictures are the only thing I took with me when I left Mogadishu. I keep them framed, hanging above my bed, and I will see you there until we meet again somewhere in this world.

Much love and God bless you all!

Your friend,

Najma Hussein

The Old Normal

Najma Hussein

I grew up in Mogadishu, which is the capital of Somalia. It was normal to hear gunshots once or twice a day. A bomb would go off at least every week. Al-Shabaab, a jihadist fundamentalist group aligned with al-Qaeda, arrived in the city around 2009 and nothing after that was safe. It was normal for my friends and family to be temporarily displaced within the city as we scrambled for safety. We would stay at neighbors' homes during times of increased conflict or instability, depending on where the fighting was happening that day. We tried to carry on as usual, but for the last three years we lived there, it was impossible for us to go to school. It wasn't safe to go out. My father brought everything home to us so we wouldn't need to go out.

My family finally fled Mogadishu in 2013. By then the city was nearly empty and most of our neighbors had left. My mom decided that we had to go. She went first and was resettled in the United States. We would go to Ethiopia then, hopefully, be reunited with our mother in the United States. Leaving that house in Mogadishu was the only hope we had.

Our house was big and beautiful. It had six rooms, two bathrooms, and a kitchen. I shared a bedroom with my older sister. It had two windows and a bathroom attached to it. There was a large garden in the back where we grew everything we could possibly eat, it seemed like. We had tomatoes, mangoes, potatoes, limes, lemons, watermelon, all sorts of lettuce, and all the spices we needed for cooking.

I will remember our house as beautiful. But when we left, it had pockmarks from gunshots and was destroyed by war.

How I Wish

Maryam Husseyn

How I wish my country would have peace.

No more war, no more hatred, no more enemies.

That my family memories could have gone on and on: Living as a family in one big house. Sharing food, sharing beds, sharing laughs, siblings fighting all the time, but deep in love.

Standing side by side, going to school together. Children playing; elders—uncles, aunties, grandma, grandpa, mother, and father— talking. Mother's "time to go to bed," while the children want to keep playing.

I wish I could stop people from killing their own people. For less than thirty dollars. In order to feed themselves. I wish I could stop women becoming widows, babies becoming orphans before they're born, mothers losing sons before they become men, graduate students dying on the best day of their life, families losing three people at the same time.

I wish I could rescue children from the streets where they are beaten and barely surviving without anyone to take care of them. I wish I could take care of them all.

That things would go from worse to better, killing to loving, hating to helping. That people would hear the cry of injustice and see the truth.

I wish every question could be answered, every wrong righted, every dream realized, every heart and mind filled with love.

That I could have lived all my life in my beautiful country. No need to learn another language, no discrimination, no hate. Same culture, same clothes, same people, same language, understanding each other.

Kismayo

Maryam Husseyn

Kismayo!
The precious land where I was fortunate to be born
The weaving sound of the sea that was next to our home
The bird sound of the sun rising next to our home
The smooth sound of morning prayer
From the mosque next to our home

Kismayo!
How can I not miss the most beautiful city in my home country
The celebration that my family had when I was born
The neighbors and relatives who welcomed me
The big town house my dad built for his family
The excitement that we could call it "our new home"

Kismayo!
The colors of the gardens in front and back
The red and green of apples
Ripe mangos, bananas, lemons, chilies
Big in my heart
Small memories of our home

Kismayo!
I know things have changed
Good to bad
Never wanted this to happen to you, my land
I was eager to grow up with you and live my whole life there
With the Indian ocean that's on your side
But time didn't let it happen

Kismayo!
I don't forget you
Another bomb explodes
The dead and injured counting
I wish I could stop the people who killed so many
of your family and drove us away
Don't forget the people who still love you

Kismayo!
I may not have grown up with you
But I am proud to speak out for you
People have made a bad image of you
"The terrorist land, the death city, the unsafe place"
This is not the truth

Kismayo!
I believe that what they haven't seen
What they think they know
Is far different from who you are
I miss you, my land, I really do
I hope we will meet again sooner or later

A Letter to Myself
When I Was Twelve

Zamzam Nur

Dear Twelve-Year-Old Me,

I'm writing to tell you that you are about to have a rude awakening and immense culture shock! Before July 14, 2014, you lived in your safe little bubble oblivious to what was going on in other countries, and even to what was going on around you. That will change: you're moving to Somalia.

Throughout your journey, you will be faced with three things: Finding your passion, learning your culture, and most important, finding a sense of identity.

Before going to Somalia, you enjoyed reading and sitting in front of the TV. You spoke to your parents in English when they spoke to you in Somali, though they insisted that you speak Somali, so you wouldn't lose your culture. You saw the regret in their eyes: regretting coming to America to get a better life, only to have their children, having perfectly assimilated into American society, deny anything to do with Somalia. You blissfully ignored your parents' wishes for you to learn Somali culture because you were already comfortable in America. You know all this. Well guess what? Fearing their children and grandchildren wouldn't know where they came from, your parents bought a one-way ticket to Mogadishu.

Coming off the plane, you won't know what to expect. You are already sad from having left everything you ever knew behind you, so you are going to think, "What could be worse?" You will be greeted in the airport by a family member you never knew you had. Your great-uncle works at the broken-down airport and because of him, you will be able to safely and efficiently get out of there.

People say first impressions are everything, and seeing the rubble that they called an airport and the starving people outside (hoping to catch a glimpse of those rich and lucky enough to be able to go on an airplane, asking for pocket change) is going to break your heart.

You will be escorted to a bus owned by another uncle you didn't know existed. Throughout your journey in Somalia, other family members you haven't heard of will help you learn the culture, language, and religion. Without their kind and warm welcomes, you would be nowhere. Appreciate these people.

While in Somalia you will find your passion: helping those in need and helping restore Somalia to its former glory. You sort of know you want to be a doctor, but the experiences you will have in Somalia will make this a certainty. You will see things a twelve-year-old shouldn't see. You will see people dying because they cannot afford to go to the hospital. You will see those who are lucky enough to go to the hospital die at the hands of inexperienced doctors. This will enrage you, and you'll dedicate your high school career to achieving what you need to achieve to reach your goal.

Finding your identity will become the most important part of the trip. Living in Somalia for two years will help you realize who you are. No matter how American your accent sounds or how smart you are in school (don't worry: you'll be a mostly straight-A student), there will be people who will never accept you. There will still be people you encounter while grocery shopping who mutter, "immigrants," even though you were born in Minneapolis, Minnesota. You will find that you are a Somali girl as much you are an American girl, born in America, who wants to do everything in her power to restore her other, broken country.

Sincerely,
Your future self,

Zamzam

Did We Pass, Mom?

Nimo Kasim

One day we went, seven of us including my mom, to the interview place in Ethiopia. People were waiting outside, and it was the most crowded and loudest place that I have ever been. We were all holding my mom's dress, so that we wouldn't get separated from each other or lost. We were in the line, the sun on top of our heads, it was really hot, then our names were called. My mom told us to stay close. The door was narrow and a lot of people were standing and yelling to go inside. My mom tried to go through, we were still hanging on her dress. Some of us lost our shoes, but we made it inside. We were safe. We got to sit down.

"Why did you leave your homeland?"

"Because of the civil war in Somalia."

"How old are you?"

"I am nine."

"Why are you here?"

"We are trying to find peace."

And so on. After two days my mom went to get the result: pass or fail. When she came back, we were so excited that there might be someplace safe we could call home that we ran to her as soon as we saw her. Did we pass the interview, mom?

Yes. They'd given us the card that proved we were eligible to stay at the refugee camp, a place that provided free food, shelter, and more. We started school right away. We were happy that we finally had a place to settle in. Little did I know that I would move again. My family and I lived in that refuge for about seven years, and then we moved here, to America.

Best Memories

Nada Kasim

I left my country because of a civil war. Not knowing which path to follow, my mom took me and my six siblings away from Somalia. I was a five-year-old daughter who didn't have "war" in her vocabulary. Families lost loved ones, fled to other countries, unwilling to return to their land. Because of persecution or fear of persecution, families became refugees, looking for peace in Kenya, Ethiopia, Djibouti, and many other countries.

Ethiopia was my family's temporary destiny: peace, love, unity, and friendship, no rich people, no poor, everyone getting almost the same thing (three meals a day). I started school as a refugee, lived there for seven years, made my best friends, my best memories

Carolina's Song

Nimo Kasim

When we were in Aw-barre, the refugee camp, there was a lady. She used to come three or four times a year and bring us things that we needed. Her name was Carolina, and all the refugee people liked her. She had blond hair and arrived in a United Nations Human Rights Council car. Carolina walked with us and talked with us and had Somali henna on her hands. She brought blankets, forks, plates, knives, and pillows for sleeping.

We were so happy when she came, everyone would come together and dance and sing the song we made up for her:

> *Way nootimi mama Karolina hobaloo*
> *Way nootimi mama Karolina hobaloo*
> *Way nootimi mama Karalinee hobaloooo*
> *Waa noo marti yee meel ha loo yeeloo*

This translates as:

> *Mama Carolina came to us hobaloo (ho-bah-low)*
> *Mama Carolina came to us hobaloo*
> *Mama Carolina came to us hobaloooo*
> *She is our guest, let's welcome her*

The objects Carolina gave to us were special. We called them "Carolina's fork" or "Carolina's blanket," even though they were ours to keep. We still have many of these things with us here in the United States.

The Time I Left the Place Where I Spent My Childhood for a Place Where Everything Was Different

Nadifo Kasim

You are always one decision away from a totally different life.

There were about eleven thousand people living in a small town in Ethiopia and we all knew each other. Everyone who lived there had fled from civil war in their home country and found peace in this small town. My family and I moved there in November of 2007. We took a bus to a different world. I remember my mom telling us to hold onto her, in order not to lose each other. The oldest of my siblings was ten and the youngest was two.

Our new home was such a small town that in your everyday living you could see almost everyone. We went to the same big school, hospital, and market. Neighbors were as close as family. If one family needed something the others did not hesitate to help them out. I lived there with my mom, my grandma, my three uncles, six siblings, and a great grandma who passed away in 2013. This was where I made my best memories and best friends.

What We Had

Nada Kasim

I might not have lived in a fancy house, but at least I was under a roof that covered our heads, from sun, rain, possibly anything.

I might not have had a lot of clothes, but when I got a new dress once, after a long time, I was happier than I ever am when I get them easily.

I might not have had a faucet where the water is running, but I tasted every drop of water I drank after the long queue in the morning.

I might not have had a TV with a large screen, but the TV with the small screen was fun, when families and neighbors watched shows together.

I might not have had a blanket of my own in cold weather, but I felt warmer when I shared it with my sisters and brothers.

I might not have had a room of my own, but the room we shared made our family closer.

I might not have gone to a big school, but we students were tighter and became family with time.

I might not have had the best things to eat every day, but special food on the holidays tasted better.

I might not have had a fitness gym, but I walked almost everywhere and didn't need it.

I might have missed my home country, but at least I wasn't afraid of losing the people I love.

Refuge:
A Conversation
about Life in the Camp

Nadifo, Nada, Nimo, and Najma Kasim

Nada: We didn't think of ourselves as refugees in the camp. Maybe it was because we were younger. We didn't feel poor or like we lacked anything. We just ate whatever we wanted.

Najma: I didn't feel that I was a refugee. I didn't think someone was helping me. It was my best life there, but now that I am older, I wouldn't want to be there at this age.

Nada: Maybe my uncle, who was five years older than us, felt different. But when I was younger everything was perfect. You didn't have to worry about what you were going to eat. All the older people thought about that.

Nadifo: Our mother didn't love life in the camp.

Nada: But I've never seen her sad. Even there. Even when she didn't know what was going to happen to us or where we were going to end up. She worked hard for us and still does.

Najma: But being kids, it was the life. When we left the refugee camp, I was so sad. I didn't want to leave.

We Learned the Hard Way
Not to Take Water For Granted

Najma Kasim

In the refugee camp, we lacked basic necessities, such as water, food, clothing, shelter, and jobs. The monthly rations per person consisted of cereals, legumes, vegetable oil, sugar, salt, famix*, and 100 birr cash, or approximately 6 US dollars. The UNHCR (United Nations High Commissioner for Refugees) also provided gasoline for the lanterns we used for light at night.

The food wasn't enough for one meal a day.

The shelter didn't protect us from too hot or too cold. When we first moved to the camp, we were given large flat bags and long pieces of wood to build the shelter we would sleep in that same night, and every night. It wasn't safe, because we didn't have an actual door for the first week. We used a blanket and set a heavy rock on it. We could hear hyenas roaring close by. My grandmother used to sew clothing over the bags, so it would stay warmer inside. This was home. Though the bag-roof disintegrated in the sun after a couple of months.

When we arrived, the UN gave us little trees to plant around our home. We planted about ten of them and, after some years, when the trees grew, we used to go under them to play games like hide and seek and jump rope; to cool down when it was hot out; to sit and have conversations with the neighbors, drinking Somali tea, my grandmother telling us stories. We had the tallest trees of our neighbors.

Water, the most essential resource in life. In the refugee camp, getting water was the hardest thing of all. Every morning we woke up early to get in a line with a couple of twenty-liter bottles and wait for the water to come. Sometimes the water wouldn't come for weeks. People would walk to the nearby town to buy bottles of water, which were very expensive. There were no jobs in the camp, whether you were educated or not.

---

* A supplementary food for young children and pregnant and lactating mothers.

When the water doesn't come, when you don't have water to cook with, or to wash your clothes with, or simply to drink, you realize the importance of water. We all learned the hard way not to take water for granted. When there was water, we said *alhamdulillah* for what we got.

Now that I am safe, I prefer not to remember. I am just glad that we got this chance. I hope that I can help people who live the way I used to, in the camp.

What We Brought to America

Nimo Kasim

1. Three Holy Books from our home in Somalia

2. Each of our First through Seventh year school certificates

3. *Uunsi** made by my grandma

4. Perfumes that my grandma also made for us

5. A couple of Islamic books we used to study with back home

6. A photo album

7. A dictionary, Somali to English

8. An English grammar book

9. Two English textbooks. I remember hating them when we lived in Aw-barre. I couldn't understand them! Now I look back at them and laugh at how easy they were.

10. A *baati†* that my grandma used to wear. When she washed it, it got shorter, so she gave it to me. I wore it when I was in Minnesota and now my sister Nada wears it most of the time. Every time she wears it, it reminds me of my grandma standing in front of me.

---

* A type of incense rock, made of incense combined with white copper and sugar. Nimo's grandmother made it in the refugee camp and would sell it there.

† A Somali dress with a long, fluid, wide-sleeved silhouette.

Adapting

Nadifo Kasim

One day my mom started packing up everything and I got like about twelve shots for vaccination. Here it comes, the last day that I stepped my legs in Africa, Tuesday, July 8th, 2014.

I left the friends I went to school with and played jump rope with. It was the worst feeling that I have ever felt in my whole life. (Now, what I miss the most is fighting with my friends over simple things and forgiving each other five minutes later.) I still can see, when I close my eyes, the last glimpse of my friends, neighbors, family, my grandma waving at us.

I went to the airport with my mom, my six siblings, and six huge bags. It was the longest two days of my life, in an airplane or waiting for an airplane. I couldn't sleep that night on the airplane. The one from Ethiopia stopped in Frankfurt, Germany. The next airplane landed in New York in the late afternoon of a Thursday, July 10th, 2014. The case worker came and told us we were going to take a car to Hartford, Connecticut. She was Somali, but she couldn't speak Somali very well. The driver was an Arab man—I remember Mom and him talking Arabic. He bought some fruit and chips. We were very hungry because the food at the airport was different from what we used to eat, so we hadn't eaten any. After we had the snacks, my siblings and I slept on each other in the car. When we got to Hartford Mom woke us up and we carried our bags and supplies to the apartment. It was a three-bedroom apartment and it was three AM. We all lay down and slept right there, our first sleep in America.

We didn't know anyone in Connecticut and didn't know where to start, so we only stayed for about a week, then all seven of us took a bus to Minneapolis where my aunt Fatoun lived. I remember we woke up very early, ate breakfast, and the case worker took us to the bus station in New York. I remember the men putting the bags in the baggage hold complained that we had too many bags, they would only take one. My mom told us to take the bags on the bus with us. Later on, another man stopped us, weighed our bags, and took money. That first bus stopped in Philadelphia late at night. We waited for the next bus. We were going by the numbers and names written on the ticket. If we didn't understand, we showed our bus tickets to people and they pointed—when the time came and the screen said the number of the bus and "Columbus, Ohio," we lined up. I remember the window seats were all taken. There were no open seats together and we had to sit individually with other people.

I remember it was cold at night. We weren't wearing jackets and we didn't have blankets. In Chicago we got on another bus to Minneapolis, where our aunt met us at the station.

This trip took two nights and three days.

Our first night in Minnesota, we stayed at our aunt's place. For four months after that we lived in a place, called Mary's Place, where they help newcomers. They helped my mom find a job and a house. My aunt showed us how to pay the rent, and basically how to do everything we didn't know how to do to adapt to American life. Since we didn't have a car, we used to ride the city bus. My mom also used the city buses and trains to get to work.

We lived in Minneapolis for a year before we moved to Green Bay, Wisconsin.

Here I am. I am not planning to move again any time soon.

America the Annoying, Painful, and Amazing

Hafsa Husseyn

I am a young Muslim woman from Africa, by way of a refugee camp in Kenya since my family was forced out of Somalia by war. When I first came to the United States, I experienced hardships and ease at the same time. I didn't want to fit in if it meant giving up my language, clothing, religion, and perspective, but I wanted so badly to be accepted into this new society. In the beginning I felt like an outsider. I met different people with different cultures, religions, and languages that were all new to me. There were times where I would cry because I felt lost and just wanted answers to the unknown. The hardest thing was going to a new school where I didn't know anyone or anything about the requirements and expectations. It was nerve wracking to adapt to something that didn't feel real.

It was also amazing. I experienced snow for the first time. (In Africa we had heat waves and warm rain.) I remember the first snow day: I wore flip flops and no jacket. The touch of the snow was cold, and it melted right in my hand. I slipped a few times on the road and fell into puddles, which was more annoying and painful than amazing.

I am a young Muslim woman from Africa who has seen struggle and pain, and here in America I am different. I wear a veil. I must prove to people that I am dedicated to working hard and reaching goals we all understand, like freedom, shelter, and safety, like learning and making things better. Seeing my mother struggle to bring my siblings and me to a better place gave me power and hope. I plan to work with people who are as unfortunate as I was. I hope to change people's stereotypes about me. The essence of diversity is having different cultures, backgrounds, and beliefs and still embracing one another for our uniqueness and our skills.

The First Winter

Bisharo Abdullahi

The first time it snowed, we were in North Carolina. I was seventeen and I was waiting for my bus to school. Snow was coming, but I didn't know that. I'm from Djibouti! There's no snow in Djibouti. It's hot. You're sweating all day.

Waiting for the bus that day it was cold, I was wearing sandals, and the bus was taking a long time. It's supposed to come at 7 AM, and I had been waiting, in my sandals, since 6:30. I had to make sure I was there early because I had to catch the bus. If I didn't catch the bus, I'd have to stay home the whole day. There was no one to drive me.

It was so cold at the bus stop that I wondered if this was the end of the world.

The bus finally came, and we finally got to school, but I was a nervous wreck. In my classroom, instead of sitting down, I stood there, and I started crying.

The teacher asked what I was doing.

My face felt frozen and it was hard to talk. I said, "I'm cold! Can't you see?"

When she saw the tears, she apologized. Then she noticed my sandals. "You're supposed to wear socks in the cold," she told me. "Wear two pairs of socks."

After school, a friend took me shopping and I got shoes for winter, boots.

At home I told my mom it was so cold I had cried.

The next day we stayed home because it was snowing and in North Carolina, they don't go to school or work if there's too much snow. It's not like Wisconsin.

Now I know how to prepare myself. Now I drive in the snow. I am used to it, but I still wear two pairs of socks.

Foods That We
(Or at Least Some of Us)
Love Here:

chocolate
ice cream
chocolate
Flamin' Hot Cheetos
cheese pizza
all-you-can-eat restaurants (My mother says to eat the healthy stuff
first. I say, but then I won't have room for the good stuff.)
Indian food
cheeseburgers

Foods That
We Miss Here:

pasta like it was in Somalia (It's the same as here, but the water we boil
it in tastes different, so the pasta tastes different.)
fresh ginger
really fresh meat
camel milk (delicious with rice for breakfast)
anjero (similar to sourdough crepes)
beer iyo basa (camel or goat liver and onions)

Green Bay

Najma Kasim

I moved here just four years ago, but I feel like I've been here all my life. At first we kept moving. Not only cities, but homes. We lived in shelters. I never felt settled. I felt like I didn't have a home.

When we moved to Green Bay, I knew I wanted to live the rest of my life here. Even though they don't understand me or the hijab I'm wearing, Green Bay still tries.

When I first came to Green Bay, it was summer. I didn't know anybody. I felt odd and lonely. Because I wear a hijab and don't speak English very well, I used to think that I'd never talk to anyone. I knew my life would be hard here. There were not many Somali or Muslim people. I had expected more, expected to make many friends. I thought I would find a friend who spoke the same language. But here, I had to make friends in English.

Now I am the one who is making others understand: who I am, where I come from, and what the hijab means to me. I explain and explain. Repeat. Again and again. But I am getting somewhere. Green Bay is my home now. It is peace. It is quiet. It is small, but it doesn't matter. It is a real hometown.

New Girl

Bisharo Abdullahi

I like to keep busy. I plow the snow in front of my house and scrape the snow off my father's and sister's cars, or I read a book, or write—I don't like doing nothing. I don't like feeling bored.

I want to learn as fast as I can, learn about things I never saw before, and how to pronounce them. I like to talk to my friends by writing email or texting. It helps me learn how to spell new words. Maybe it is not good to talk to your friends too much when you're at school, but sometimes it makes your day happy.

When I came to America my whole life changed. Everything was new to me—people, food, weather, language, and even time—and I became a new person.

What's Different Here:

Rain. Here the rain smells bad. In Somalia, rain smells wonderful.

Flavors. We can make the same food that we used to, but the food tastes different here. Tea tastes different: the cinnamon, cloves, sugar, and ginger we use in tea taste different too.

Sardines. They used to be my favorite thing. I want to get very rich so I can travel the world and buy all the sardines in cans because here they don't taste as good.

Time. In Somalia, there were so many mosques, you always knew what time it was by the prayer bells. And the sun was always in the same position at the same time, so it was always the same amount of daylight at the same time every day.

This Is What You Should Tell Someone Who Is Coming to America

Nimo Kasim

Meeting people you don't know
Eating food you never ate before
Standing at the bus station
Waiting for the bus to come
Trying to speak words you don't know
Learning new things
Going to new school
Wearing big shoes and jackets in the winter

Bittersweet

Nadifo Kasim

Coming from Africa to the United States was bitter. But it is sweet that now I feel safe every time I am sleeping.

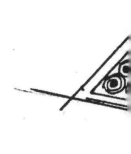

Family

Where I'm From

Najma Hussein

I am from the family picture with long dresses and hijab,
>From the duplex house white with black brick,
It smelled like cinnamon.
I am from the buttercup flowers in the yard,
>From the guava tree from my grandma,
>From the spaghetti on holiday and light skin.
I am from Mohammed, Mahmoud, Ayan, Najib, and Ahmed,
>From staying up late at night and sleeping all day.
I am from "Stay out of trouble" and "insha'Allah."*
>From the Quran, the Sunnah, and the *masjid*,
I am Somalian, Arabian. Goat meal and camel milk.
I am from the time that Najma and Ayan decided to eat the whole pizza
And the day of silliness,
>From the family photo hanging in the living room,
>From the blue flag with the white star.

---

* "God willing"

Sisters

Nada Kasim

Sisters are different flowers from the same garden. I have four.

My super-organized sister is the one that I don't get to touch her clothes. If we want to borrow something, we have to make a deal like doing her homework or washing the dishes. If the rest of us are doing laundry on Saturday, she does hers on Sunday, so that our clothes don't get mixed up. She knows where every single one of her possessions is and notices what is missing. Sharing a room with her isn't the easiest thing in the world. Once I wore one of her dresses and she made my day miserable. After that I vowed never to borrow her stuff. Even though I don't like it when she doesn't share, I've still learned many things from her that will help me in the future, like when I'm living in a dorm with my roommates in college.

Another sister is my best friend. This is the sister that I go to when I need advice or have two options and don't know which one to choose. We like the same outfits, movies, music, and the same types of people. She cooks the things I like whenever she makes food for the family. She helps me out and defends me when my mom is mad at me, like the time I lost my phone and my mom refused to buy me a new one, this sister took my side. I still don't know how she convinced my mom that day, but I got the phone, so I thanked her from the bottom of my heart.

I look up to the sister who is good at everything. She is like a second mom, so leading and protective, so precocious that my parents trust her the most even though she is not the oldest. I never see her sad or crying. This sister doesn't play with us much and it is rare to find her sitting and not doing anything. She likes working and cleans the house. She says that she is uncomfortable in the house when it is not clean. She is the trustworthy, perfect sister. I love her.

Then there is the sister who thinks I am annoying. This sister likes nothing about me. She finds me a stranger and thinks everything I do is weird. She is one year younger than me, almost the same height. We have totally different opinions and ideas. We don't agree about almost anything and she is always the opposite of me. It is hard to sleep with her in the same room because she sets the alarm to ring every five minutes and since she doesn't wake up easily, I have to wake up and turn off the alarm. One stormy day this sister and I ended up staying home by ourselves. We kept fighting over the television, but eventually we found a comedy movie that we both liked and spent the night laughing and crying because we were laughing so hard. When she isn't home I miss her and the house feels empty without her, because I don't have someone to argue with. It doesn't matter how much she bothers me, I can't imagine my life without her.

My sisters and I have always lived under the same roof. We don't always get along, but my life would not be complete without them. After all, they are my small world.

Hooyo (Mommy)

Nadifo Kasim

She is kind
She is caring
She is loving and charming
She is my best friend
She is a rose
Hooyo

Hooyo
You mean the world to me
You taught me how to walk step by step
You are the ink of my pen
I am who I am today
Because of you
Hooyo

Hooyo
I feel safe and happy whenever I see you
I feel you on my shoulder everywhere I go
Hooyo

Hooyo
You are the best hooyo
Every time I want something
You understand me without my telling you
Give me everything without asking
What would I do without you?
Hooyo

Hooyo
Your smile means
Everything
My sweet life
Would be tasteless without you

If I keep thanking until
The last second of my life
I can't thank you enough
Hooyo

Hooyo
I know
You think about
Us ten times more
Than you think about
Yourself
Hooyo

Hooyo
You're more than
Just an ordinary hooyo
When you wait for all
Your seven children
To sit at the table
Before you start eating
Hooyo

Hooyo
What can I do
To repay you
Hooyo

A Photo from Before

Nimo Kasim

When I look at my favorite photo, I see how young I was. Also, how young my siblings were at that time. I see a white house behind us. There was a red car in front of that house. I hear the many people who were laughing and walking next to us, wearing new clothes; cars honking to each other as they passed. We were happy because it was Eid al-Adha.

I see my six younger siblings. Two of my sisters stand to my left. The others sit on chairs, my youngest brother in front of me. I have my hands on his shoulder, he and I in matching gray and white. Two of my younger sisters are wearing jackets and pants. All my siblings have their heads uncovered. Only I wear a hijab. I guess this is because I am the oldest, but I remember it was my choice. Since I was a baby, I never liked showing my hair.

We aren't smiling, except my youngest brother. You can see his teeth very well. We didn't yet have the Refugee Card. When we got it, we moved to a safe place, Aw-barre Refugee Camp. We were happy there.

Ayeeyday Canab
Qofka aan Ugu Jecelahay Aduunka

Nada Kasim

Ayeeyo...
Ayeeyo...
Ayeeyo...
Waan kuu xiisayoo
Rajadaydu waxay tahay
Habeen iyo maalin
Inaan kulano sida ugu dhakhsaha badan
Iiga sheekaysid sheeko dheeroo
Xirfada ku jirta aad ii sheegtid dabateed
Hooyaday markay tiraahdo
Nimo, Najma, yish...
Nasteexo, yish... Nadifo, Nada
Adaan ku soo xasuustaayoo
Markaasaan dhahaa
"Naa ballaayo kaalay"
Waa sidday ayeeyday dhihi jirtay
Markay magacyadaayada kala saari wayso
Masaafada noo jirta badanaa
Laakiin qalbigaan kugu hayaayoo
Laba guriyoo daris ah masaafada u jirta
Aniga agtayda nooma dhaxayso
Allah... maxaan u xiisay
Wajigaaga nuurkiisa
Qalbigaaga dahabka ah
Sheekooyinkaaga xirfada leh
La'aantaa inaan noolaado
Dhib bay igu tahayoo
Rajaydaydu waxay tahay
Inaan kuu shaqeeyoo
Xajka ku geeyo
Inkastoon abaalkaaga gudi karin
Waxaad agtayda ka tahay Hooyo

Hooyo macaan, Ayeeyo macaan
Abaalkaaga magudi karee
Qalbigayga waxaad ku leedahay in wayn
Waxaad ibartay
Khaldka, saxda, iyo faraqoodaa
Qayrkay saan uga sarayn lahaa
Adiga dartaa ayaan u ahay
Qofka aan ahay maanta
Xasuustaada waa igu qaaliyoo
Maalin ima dhaafto
Anigoo kaa fikirin
Ama qalbiga ku haynin waanadaada
Adaan kuugu jecelahay aduunkoo
Allaha na jamciyo anagooo khayr qabna
Allaha tacabkaaga ha khasaarininoo
Oo iga dhig sawirka aad ku sawiratay
Maskaxdaada anigoo ah mustaqbalka
Hooyo macaan, Ayeeyo macaan
Kawnka adaan kuugu jeclahayee
Allaha iikaa dhawrsho

My Grandma Anab
The Person I Love Most in the World

Ayeeyo...
Ayeeyo...
Ayeeyo...
I miss you
Every night and every day
My hope is to see you again
As soon as possible
So that you can tell me a long, inspiring story.

When my mom says
Nimo, Najma, aaah...
Nasteho, aaah... Nadifo, Nada...
I recall what you used to say:
Come on naa ballaayo
Come on whatever your name is
Is what Ayeeyo used to say
When she got confused about our names
As they all start with N.

The distance between us
Is from the middle of the world
To the very west of the world
But in my heart...
The distance between us
Is closer than two neighbor houses.

Oh, Ayeeyo, no one can imagine
How much I miss your brightful face
Your like-gold face
Your stories.

My dream is to have a decent job
To work…
So that I can take you to the Hajj
Even though I cannot thank you enough.

Ayeeyo, to me
You are more than Grandma
You are my sweet mother
Who I love most in the world.

May Allah make us meet soon
May I become how you raised me to be
May I become the picture
You imagined of me in the future
May Allah bless you and keep you safe.

I'll always have you in my heart
Until the last day of my life.

Beautiful Family

Nimco Sh. Abdullahi Hassan

My mother has this foster daughter—my mom raised her, she doesn't know any other parents. She and my mom have a very beautiful relationship. I consider her my big sister. She came to the United States from our hometown, Qabribayax, before us, by herself, and helped guide us through everything. She was the other hand of my mom after the loss of my father.

From America, my big sister supported us back home as we struggled in a refugee camp while she got a better college education for herself. I have never met anyone that strong. I am blessed to call her my big sister, blessed to look up to her. I love her so much. What my sister has done as a grownup woman makes me think I can do the same, not only for my family, but for the many families in need. I believe that if you love your family and help raise them up, you have helped a humanity as a whole. We might each have our own family, but we are one.

My big sister's name is Fadha. She has always been the one that understood me best. I go to her with everything. My mom can't understand everything that's going on with my life, but my big sister can. I have a beautiful family.

A Letter to Aunt Fatoun

Dear Habo Fatoun Ali,

You are a role model with a beautiful heart and contagious smile. You cheer up everyone around you. When we first met you, we didn't know you. But we felt an immediate connection, sensed that you were the one. You, more than anyone, would help us through the struggles we would face as newcomers.

We thank you, Habo Fatoun, for making us feel at home. You welcomed us with an open heart and we remember the joyful moments we shared with you and your family. You became part of our family. Now, festival celebrations like birthday parties, graduations, Ramadan, and Eid don't feel complete without you. You showed us how to get around, and your home became our second home.

Habo, you inspire us and make us smile. Without you, we would never have seen the world as we do now or taken the next steps in our lives. You were there for us when we felt alone, scared, and confused, you stepped up and guided us to overcome obstacles and follow our dreams. You encouraged us to keep going forward through battles in life, particularly education. You introduced us to other great and helpful people. We love you so much and we can't thank you enough. We miss you and our cousins, Hanad, Hibo, Hanan, and Harun. You are the greatest gift we've ever received.

Sincerely,

The Kasim Sisters

I Like to Listen to Both Sides

Najma Kasim

One day, at my neighbor's house, there was a little girl whose mother accused her of nearly burning down the house. Her mother came back from work and started yelling at her, even though she hadn't given her daughter a chance to explain herself. Later, I asked the girl what had happened, and she told me that her little brother was about to burn himself with a candle. To save her brother she threw the candle and the candle burned the house. Her mom yelled at her without knowing the whole truth. After that day, I decided to listen to people before I make any big decisions.

The Given and the Taken

Maryam Husseyn

Seven years we waited for a visa
Then four flights and two and half days
And we landed
In the greatest country.

Three months in Minnesota
Then to Green Bay
And we struggled
In the new country.

A new house, new schools, new jobs
Then Alhamdulillah, Praise God, it went well
And I was proud to call
The new country, the greatest country, my second home.

November 11, 2014
One little angel, my sister's first born
Then he came home
And he was welcomed
In unimaginable happiness.

Countless blessings for our family, Alhamdulillah
Then every day he waited at the door
And he greeted us
In shining cuteness.

One little aunt and best friend, me
Then he was a little naughty, but funny as well
And he called us all *Hooyo*
Which means "Mom" in Somali.

Many good memories,
Then, for a few months, he had not been well
And his skin turned pale
And dark spots appeared under his eyes
And he lost most of his appetite
And he was weak and fragile
In sickness.

May 31, 2017
Three days before my high school graduation
Then he was rushed to the hospital
And they couldn't do anything for him
In their uncertainty about what was wrong.

The third night he was transferred to Milwaukee Children's Hospital
Then he was two hours from Green Bay
And a month and half later he was still there
And he was treated for typhoid
And the nights turned into days
And his sickness progressed
While we worried.

For days he was unconscious
Then suddenly he went blind
And the doctors were confused
In the room where my nephew lay helpless.

Stage four lymphoma cancer, the worst news
Then a month of chemo
And he was brave
And his eyesight came back
And he could talk and play again
And see his family with his own eyes
And we rejoiced
In this gift.

One year in and out of the hospital
Then things changed
And my nephew is no longer with us
Since he was chosen by Allah, our creator.

Four years old, four years loved
Then he was taken
And nonetheless I am grateful
In my sorrow, in my grief, in my faith.

Everything Allah does for us
Then, too, everything he has promised
And "Allah does not fail on his promise"
In his infinite concern for us.

Every day this little boy lived with pain
That he couldn't understand or share
Terrible, but we can still be grateful
Knowing this world was created
Not to make us happy every day
Rather to make us work for the hereafter.

Neverending happiness in that eternal place
No death, nor pain, nor struggle or depression
Allah, The Creator, The sustainer
Gives us life, takes us back, and tests us in between
For patience, the key to paradise.

I'm Learning to Drive

Nimco Sh. Abdullahi Hassan

I live with my mom and my two little sisters. My mom does not know how to drive. My brothers are scared for her—they don't want her to drive because she takes care of us all by herself since my dad passed away. She sometimes has a hard time. She gets distracted. When she wants to get groceries or do laundry, I'm the one that helps her. She needs me to drive, and I need to drive for myself, too. So, I'm learning to drive.

Dear Dad

Nada Kasim

Baba...

As kids, when we saw our friends with their dads, our hearts got broken again and again. Hearts in pieces, the missing piece was you. All the years that you were not beside us, we dreamed of seeing you, listened to mom telling us stories about you, the perfect dad that we pictured in our heads. You were close and far, your voice traveling thousands of miles by phone.

The blessed day you came in person was a day of mixed emotions: nervousness, happiness, curiousness. Standing in front of you at the airport, in the moment that we had waited for: joy, disbelief, and other words we couldn't think of. We didn't know how to express our feelings to you. How to describe the warmth of the first hug after eleven years?

It might have been awkward saying *Aabo** so many times a day, in the days after our reunion, but we had saved up a lot of questions. Little by little, we are getting to know you again. We are putting our hearts back together and, *alhamdulillah*, finally our family is complete.

Love,

Your daughters

---

*   *Baba* and *aabo both* mean "dad."

My Mom

Najma Kasim

My mom is my world.

Every day and night I like to put a smile on her face. My mom, she is my best friend. If I put myself in her shoes, I wouldn't be able to handle it for one second. She is very patient. Whenever I face obstacles she is there to guard and guide me. My mom is inspirational to me. Being a single mother with seven children is a lot harder than you can imagine, but my mom never let us work while we were in school. She believes we wouldn't be able to focus on both our education and our jobs. She works very hard for us to get whatever we need. She goes to work at noon, while we are at school, and when she comes home at midnight, we're asleep. When we go to school in the morning, she's asleep. On the weekends, it feels like we haven't seen each other forever.

All that I am today or hope to be in the future, I owe to my kind-hearted mom. My mom is and always has been my greatest teacher of compassion, of patience, of love, and mostly, of fearlessness.

I thank Allah for such a mother.

How They Wear This Smile

Nada Kasim

I lived in a refugee camp for about seven years, it is where I spent my childhood. There were eleven thousand of us there. The elders, my neighbors, my teachers, and my mom were my role models. They are the ones that I wanted to follow in their path of how they wear this smile, while they are in pain because they hear every single day all the horrible things that happen in the home country they fled. Also, how they wake up every morning, thinking about how they will feed their children, how they will never let us feel hunger.

I have six siblings, and I am the quietest. I can't imagine not having my brown skin, not wearing my hijab every day when I go out, and not living in a crowded house with a big family where we share almost everything.

We are the first Somali generation to settle in Green Bay.

Faith

Where I'm From

Bisharo Abdullahi

I'm from farming families,
    From a tree with many branches.
    From caring and kindness,
    From Mom and Dad.
I'm from Dad gardening in the backyard,
    From planting flowers and roses.
    From roads filled with laughter,
    From a smile filled with joy.
I'm from streets crowded with markets,
    From anjero with sauce.
I'm from Ramadan, when we fast,
    From where families gather and eat at sunset,
    From a Quran that teaches peace.
I'm from praying five times a day,
    From turning my face towards Mecca.
I'm from hot desert,
    From sandy winds.

Ramadan in America

Nadifo Kasim

Ramadan is the ninth month of the Muslim year, during which Muslims fast from sunrise to sunset. But here in Wisconsin in July the sun is still up at eight o'clock at night. My mom thought the clocks were wrong. In Africa the sun goes down at six o'clock every day of the year. We used to fast for about twelve hours, now we fast about seventeen hours a day.

Being Hijabi
(Or, Wearing a Scarf)

Nada Kasim

Being hijabi is one of the first things people notice about me. Some think that I am having a bad hair day, while others think I don't have hair at all. Some think I'm forced to wear hijab. Others assume that I am opinionated and religious, close to God. Or maybe I am dumb, as if my scarf didn't just cover my hair but also my brain. Others think that I must be a good, honest person. But the truth is that I just feel comfortable wearing hijab and it is something I choose to do.

Here's what I think: I am what I am from inside and wearing a scarf or not wearing one doesn't change me.

Can You Hear Me Through This Thing?

Nimco Sh. Abdullahi Hassan

I work at Walmart, and I see a lot of people every day. I try to be friendly with everybody because positivity is the way to go. But one day I experienced something I never thought I would experience in America, especially in Green Bay with the wonderful people here.

I was stocking groceries and a lady came up to me. She said, "Hey can you hear me through that thing?"

She was tugging on my hijab.

She said, "I don't think she can hear me! I'm speaking to a wall."

I said, "I hear you well." But the woman ignored me and kept talking.

I didn't know who to feel bad for: myself, or this person who didn't know what she was talking about.

I started crying. There were children laughing. Adults around us were saying, "She is being terrible to you, you should tell someone. She should be banned from the store." But I thought, no, I don't blame this woman. I blame the people who didn't teach her what the hijab means. It wasn't her fault, she didn't know what she was talking about. It was sad, and yes kids were laughing, but I also felt bad for her because she was ignorant.

I get my courage and my calm from my religion. It's how Muhammad (may peace be upon him) taught his people. We believe there are two angels recording what you do, good or bad. If you ignore that beautiful heart God gave you and do wrong, you don't feel good. I don't always do as well as I should, but in this incident I think I did what I've learned from Muhammad's books.

The woman was older. I wanted to be respectful. I couldn't talk back to her. So I tried to give her a little bit of knowledge.

I told her about the hijab and why I wore it and under what circumstances I take it off. She quickly became embarrassed and started crying, too. She said, "Oh my God! I was making fun of you and now you're trying to teach me something. I am so sorry."

She told me, "Now I know why people wear this. I have lived in Wisconsin my whole life, and no one has ever told me what hijab is for. I only know what CNN says. I only know about terrorists. But this is a religious piece."

She said, "It's like what Catholic sisters wear."

In my diversity classes, we talk about discrimination and prejudice and social stratification. This was a real example. The woman just didn't get the knowledge she should have had.

She said she felt very bad. I told her, "I am feeling bad for myself and for you, so I am trying to give you the knowledge so you can just live, ma'am."

And she laughed.

The experience was sad for me at first, but it can happen. That's what I want to teach my little sisters and the children I will interact with when I am a social worker. I just want to teach positivity. You can't solve a problem with negativity, you have to be the person who solves it, positively. Reacting negatively takes a lot of talking and energy, and makes things worse. This woman was just telling me what she saw on CNN. She had no right to say what she said, but I feel like how I reacted to it was what she needed.

I was raging on the inside, but I chose positivity. So, I was calm on the outside. I think it was the right thing to do. We both learned something, and that's why I love people. In my career, I will be working with people from all over the world, and I want to know what makes them happy. People are beautiful and amazing. Instead of getting angry, I think educating people is the right thing to do.

The Everlasting Holiday

Nasteho Kasim

Ramadan is the most important month for Muslims everywhere. It takes place during the ninth month of the Islamic calendar, which is the month that our holy book, the Quran, was revealed to Muhammad. I look forward to Ramadan every year, and so does my family. It is the month when I feel closer to my creator, Allah, and show him my faithfulness. We fast twenty-nine or thirty days depending on the moon.

My family and all Muslims around the world increase prayers and charity during this month. In Ramadan, everyone fasts by not eating or drinking from sunrise to sunset. The old, the sick, and pregnant women don't have to fast, but they would need to give food to the poor or make it up later. The starting age for fasting is fifteen years old, though many Muslim children start younger, in my case when I was nine. I didn't fast all the hours, but the practice helped me be ready for when I would fast completely for Ramadan, which I started when I was twelve.

We Muslims fast this month not only as an act of worship, to get closer to Allah, but to help us feel empathy toward poor people all around the world. They live every day without having all three meals; for us it is only a month. Fasting is also a way to learn patience, break bad habits, and even ease anger. We consider it the best chance to seek forgiveness from Allah for all our wrong deeds. People who don't fast might view it as boring and tiring and don't seem to understand why we would fast for so long, but that's not how I see it. It's not boring or tiring to me. Ramadan is a special time because the ties between my family and with my extended family are closer than ever. At ifter (sunset), we cook special foods, and at the end of Ramadan, we celebrate the best holiday for all Muslims, Eid. At Eid we get new things and spend the whole day celebrating with family.

The Color of the Sky

Nada Kasim

As a child, I always wanted to be like my mom, aunts, and grandma and wear the hijab. I remember the first hijab that my grandma designed and gifted me when I was seven years old: the color of the hijab was the color of the sky with white flowers and it was precious to me. When we celebrated Eid, I used to compete with my friends over who would get the cutest new dress and hijab for Eid. Later, when I lived in a refugee camp, all the women covered their hair. Coming from such a place and coming to the United States, where women do not cover their heads, was new to me. When my classmates asked me about my culture and why I wear hijab, I had to ask myself. I'd never had to answer this question before.

Hijab isn't just about wearing a scarf on my head, it's about covering my body with loose clothing in order to concentrate on becoming who I am within. True hijab comes from inside, just as true modesty comes from within.

In the Qur'an, Allah tells the believers to "lower their gaze and be modest." Specifically, it says: "Say to the believing men that they should lower their gaze and guard their modesty; that will make for greater purity for them; and Allah is well acquainted with all that they do. And say to the believing women that they should lower their gaze and guard their modesty; and that they should not display their beauty and ornaments except what must ordinarily appear thereof; that they should draw their veils over their chests and not display their beauty except to their husbands, their fathers, their husbands' fathers, their sons, their husbands' sons, their brothers, their brothers' sons, their sisters' sons, their women, that which their right hands possess, or those male attendants having no physical desire, or children who are not yet aware of the private aspects of women." (Qur'an 24:30-31).

People asking me why I am wearing hijab is as weird to me as my asking them why they have not covered their hair. I believe that the hijab protects me. I can't imagine myself going out without hijab because I would feel naked. And like a different person. This is why I wear my hijab.

Finding my clothing style in the stores is almost impossible in Green Bay. Our first year in the United States, my family and I wore the clothing that we'd brought with us. My mom is the only one that works in the family. Traveling to another state to get a new hijab wasn't really an option, but we needed new clothes. That's when it occurred to me that I like design—I could make my own clothes! Teaching myself how to use the sewing machine was a challenge. YouTube, social media, and sewing websites helped. Using a simple fabric and making any style that I wanted was a dream of mine that has come true.

Whenever I finish a piece of clothing, I thank my new community, who helped me learn designing and sewing without them knowing it. It is not Green Bay's fault that it does not have my clothing style in its stores—I would not see their clothing style sold in my home country either. I've learned a skill that I will have for the rest of my life. Someday I will sell the clothing that I design to the stores where I live, which will make it easier for young Muslim girls to dress like I do without going through the same struggles. I do not regret what I went through, however, because it is a pleasure to be able to wear your own design and see others wearing it, too.

I want to be strong enough to keep up with my culture without being afraid to be isolated because of my difference. I like to always think of my difference as an advantage and not as a disadvantage. My dream is to be a successful Muslim woman who becomes absolutely wonderful in her field, while still covering up and maintaining the modesty that I choose to uphold.

I kept that first hijab that my grandmother made for me in the color of the sky. I am planning on gifting it to my first daughter.

Hijab Story

Najma Hussein

One day, in Mogadishu, my older sister and her friends went out to buy candies for the kids. They met several men on the road with machine guns in their hands. "Where is your hijab? Where are you going? You're not supposed to be out alone without a brother," asked the men with the guns.

My sister was wearing a shorter hijab which covered past her shoulders but did not provide the full coverage the men demanded. In America, Muslim women can wear any kind of scarf as long as it covers our hair. We can use other clothing to cover our bodies. According to the terrorists my sister met, from a fundamentalist East Africa-based group called al-Shabaab, women must wear a proper hijab: a long covering made of a specific fabric that only allows skin from your face and hands to show and is loose enough to not reveal the outline of your body. This isn't to say this hijab is wrong. What's wrong is men with guns insisting on it. Islam is not about forcing people to worship Allah. It gives good advice to people to spread the religion peacefully. The Quran teaches that attracting people to Islam must occur through good-mannered preaching and discussion, not by force.

The men of al-Shabaab asked many questions before they let my sister and her friends go with their first warning. If they got caught a second time they would be beaten or killed, if that is what the men with guns wished to do. Men without guns, it should be noted, have the same problems with al-Shabaab as anyone else on the roads. Men cannot cut their hair any way they like, because the terrorists will either kill them or force them to join their group.

Al-Shabaab is a terrorist group convinced that their religious beliefs are the best and the rest of us are wrong. They want to control Somalia and its people. Personally, I have never seen someone who is in this group, but I used to hear from TV and radio what was going on. I never went out without someone with me, either one of my siblings or my dad. Most of the time we were "*home children*," meaning we rarely saw outside of the house. Papa went out and brought us what we needed.

Here in the United States people believe in freedom of religion. One of the first questions I asked myself after I moved here was whether it really matters if I wear my hijab or not. And if I do wear my hijab, what will people think about me?

One day a woman asked why I am wearing this piece of cloth on my head. She did not know about Islam. I told her it is for my religion and my choice to have it on. I remember it was summer and a very hot day. She said, "Aren't you feeling hot?" There is no doubt that wearing a hijab in the summer is very, very hard, but it is a good deed and I am being dutiful to Allah, my God. So, I said to her, "I do not feel that hot when I remember the true hotness of the fire in hell."

It is hard for Muslim women living in western countries because people are judging and saying, "Go back to where you belong." I think some people forget that there is freedom of religion here. I don't always like being different, but at least I can practice my religion freely and safely here. Every community has both good and bad people in it. I have met mostly good people who don't judge the way I look and respect me just the way I am.

Dear Lord, I want to thank you for the beautiful people you've blessed me with.

A Lifetime Dream for Every Muslim

Nadifo Kasim

The Hajj is a once in a lifetime pilgrimage of Muslims to Mecca, in Saudi Arabia, that teaches lessons of unity, sacrifice, and brother-and-sisterhood. It brings the rich and the poor to the same row. For Muslims, the Hajj is the fifth and final pillar of Islam, one of five major awakenings to the real importance of life here on earth. Muslims believe this pilgrimage brings us close to each other and to Allah and cleans us from inside.

The pilgrims worship and ask forgiveness as they go together around the Kaaba, a cube-shaped building in Mecca that is the most sacred Muslim pilgrim shrine. Inside the Kaaba is the black stone believed to have been given by Gabriel to Abraham. (Muslims everywhere, every day turn in its direction when praying, not just during the Hajj.) As a pillar of Islam, the Hajj is a Muslim's compulsory duty, undertaken to show true faith.

The Hajj is an opportunity to reject evil and expel evilness from the body. After completing the Hajj, pilgrims may feel or see things differently and change their ways of life to be better, more steadfast and lawful Muslims. I believe that making this pilgrimage can give people hope that their lives will be better in the future. This hope can become confidence that they can change their lives and earn rewards in paradise after they die.

The Hajj cleanses Muslims from inside because they want to do something good from the bottom of their hearts. Before setting out, pilgrims must be in good health and not in debt or leaving a family in debt. They must not leave the neighbors hungry. They resolve petty arguments, make peace with everyone, and go in goodwill. When they return, pilgrims should continue their commitment and loyalty.

The Hajj can change people. My dream is to go with my mother and grandma. When I finish college and earn enough money, I want to see how the old, the young, the rich, the poor, people of all colors and nationalities stand shoulder to shoulder in prayer side by side.

School

Where I'm From

Nimo Hassan

I'm from home.

I'm from needing to leave,
>From wanting to sleep without worrying,
>From trying to learn in peace.
I'm from the civil war,
>From horror stories of tribalism,
>From Qabil used for evil,
>From ordinary people's houses under attack.
I'm from being afraid of my own people,
>From people being kept apart.
I'm from heartsickness,
I'm from prayers
>To my people and my old home.
I'm from freedom.

Welcome

Nada Kasim

You know what I was thinking about? If we were in Somalia and you came into our class, we would be the ones who should talk to you and be like, "Welcome," because you are new.

Everyday Schedule
for Life in Aw-Barre

Waking up at 5 AM
Praying with our family
Going to the Islamic school at 6 AM (dugsi)
Memorizing a page of Quran
Going to the teacher and
Reading it without the book (kitab)
Running back home
Eating breakfast and rushing to prepare for
School starting at 7:30 AM
Eating a snack at 10 AM
School finished at 12 PM
Coming home rushing as usual
Praying noon prayer
Eating lunch with our lovely family
Lying down a little bit or playing with our siblings
Going back to the Islamic School about 2:30 PM
Memorizing so we don't forget
Learning to write Arabic
Teacher takes us to the mosque
Which is next to the Islamic School
It is afternoon prayer
Praying with our friends and sisters
Our teacher leading the prayer (Imam)
Reading the nasheed
Which people in Medina read to our prophet
When he first went there
Coming back to our house with smiles on our faces at 4 PM
Drinking a cup of black tea that our grandma made
Preparing to go to the private school
Where we learn how to speak English
The teacher gives us twenty new words
Each day until we learn hundreds of words
Tells us to memorize before the competition

With other private schools
Tells us to stand up and
Have English conversation with other students
Home at 5 PM
Watching Indian or Turkish movies translated
Into Arabic
Praying evening prayer
Doing homework and
Preparing a page of Quran for tomorrow
Eating dinner with family
Praying night prayer
Sleeping

We miss these moments.

Survival

Hafsa Husseyn

Life turns and tunnels, getting what you need and want is a struggle. I once called Kakuma, a refugee camp, home. I expected it to be better than my first home, my warring country, but it wasn't, as it turned out. Every day was a mission for survival.

There was hunger and thirst, miles to walk for food and water. The days were long and the weather was unbearable and tomorrow was not a given. Our hearts pounded from the first darkness of night until sunrise. We were afraid to sleep in a dark place with no lock. We were afraid of the predators outside. We were a mother with four girls and no father to protect us. We lived so we learned to survive.

Every night was a nightmare, the sounds of gunshots and raped women crying. We imagined their pain. Days and nights and nights and days and the camp held us like captives. Our escape from this place was survival.

In the daylight, we dreamed of living in a better place, somewhere with good schools, a place where we didn't have to worry about tomorrow. Kakuma was a jungle filled with sorrow. We survived.

Nada

Nada Kasim

Hello,
Assalamu Alaikum,
Merhaba,
Salam,
This is Nada...
You can call me
Nade, Nado, Nadi, Naide, Nadha, Nadia, Naado.
Well,
Some of you may be thinking
Isn't nada nothing in Spanish?
But I am everything I can be
And Hey,
I'm lucky enough to be called
All these names by
Friends, family, teachers,
Or even strangers
Since I wasn't in control of
Other people's tongues—
Their ability to pronounce
My name.
As a newcomer student in high school
It bothered me how people
Pronounced my name
For the first couple of years
But then
All these names
Became me.
Like how actors change
Their names in the movies
But the difference is
I am still me.

A Conversation About School: Gym Class

Nadifo, Nada, Nimo, and Najma Kasim

Nadifo: Teachers think, like, we know American football! We never played back home, but they expect us to know.

Nada: We watch and try to figure it out. When Najma understands something she tells us, "Hey this is how they are doing it."

Najma : We stand back and watch. We teach ourselves. We don't ask the teacher to explain the games because everyone is going to look at you!

Nadifo: They have to stop the game to explain it to you!

Nimo: Everyone will say, like, "How do you not know?"

You Had No Idea
You Did Not Know

Nada Kasim

I left my country due to civil war and came to a country where I didn't understand its language, culture, and traditions. Getting used to living here in the United States was tough. Even though I studied English in Ethiopia, the English that people speak here has a totally different accent. I came here in 2014 and started my freshman year. I could hardly understand one sentence when the teachers were explaining the lessons. I read more books, watched more movies, and made friends to understand and learn English faster. And I gave double attention to my teachers to understand the tasks. I worked hard, and I will continue to work hard.

Without education, there is no light. In the country that I came from, many young boys and girls didn't go to school. The ones that went were the ones that could afford to—families had to pay money every month like rent for their children to study from first grade until they finish college. Now I think I have a precious opportunity to be educated, to become who I want to be in life and help others. My mom did everything she could for me to finish middle school before I came to the United States. I will not give up until I reach my goal. I want my mom to be proud. To me, education is learning things you had no idea you did not know.

At Home at School

Yasmin Nur

When I was younger, growing up in Minnesota, I didn't feel like I was part of a community. I always felt like the weird kid, the little girl with the hijab, even though I didn't understand why wearing a hijab was weird to other people. I grew up after 9/11, so I never really knew anything different and I never really knew why I was ostracized.

I was born in Minneapolis and I grew up in the suburbs of Minneapolis. We moved around a lot, but we never moved far. I went to elementary school and was happy, but I was always the one black girl, the one Muslim girl. No one was exactly like me.

We moved to Somalia in 2014. I hated it. I didn't like the food, how hot it was, or the culture, even though it was mine.

And then, I slowly started to like it. After about a year, I went to school. The kids at my school all came for different reasons; I came because I didn't know any Somali. I was told that the kids who would be my classmates were bad kids. My family told me not to make any friends there. I went to school expecting that they were going to knife me or something!

When I first came to class, I walked in with the principal, two hours late. The kids were sitting on benches, three on a bench with a long table. I sat down and was super quiet. Eventually, the girl next to me gave me a note in English. No one for the whole year I had been in Somalia had spoken English to me.

The note asked, "Where are you from?"

I said, "America."

She told everyone.

I thought, "Oh my gosh, now it's going to start, now I am in danger." The bad kids knew I was from America!

In the end, those girls were really sweet. They weren't bad. They gave me food and clothes. We had parties together. We became sisters. Most of the other girls were from Europe. Me and another girl, Selma, were the only girls from America. And Selma was from California, so we were already worlds apart. She may as well have been from Europe, too.

My classmates and I were different people, but we were all the same: We were kids who were Somali who were born in different countries, and grew up in different cultures, and we all felt the same way about having to move from our homes and start over in Somalia, but we somehow came together in Somalia. I felt like I'd found my people, I'd found who I was supposed to friends with. I'd found my group. Those girls were so funny, and I related to them. I've never related to anybody like that in my life.

When I moved back to America, it was really heartbreaking. I'd known these girls for two years and we were best friends. We made so much trouble bothering the teachers! We once had a water fight wearing full hijabs and long dresses. All the crazy stories we had together made me feel at home for once. I felt like America wasn't my home, even though it was. And it felt like Somalia wasn't my home, even though it was. I just felt like those girls were my home.

In the end I learned to love my countries, where I am and where I am from. I miss Somalia. But in Somalia, I missed America. I missed the TV, I missed speaking English, and I missed the kids even though I was different.

I still keep in touch with those girls, two years since I last saw them. They were my home, and you never forget home.

I hope to see them again.

A Letter
to Our Classmates

Nasteho Kasim, Maryam Husseyn,
and Nadifo Kasim

Dear Classmates,

On the first day we met, you didn't know anything about us, and we didn't know you, either.

If the situations were reversed, we hope we would have welcomed you, made you feel at home, and done what we could to make you feel comfortable. We hope we would have tried to make you feel "seen," not invisible. That's the kind of reception we would want for anyone, but nothing was how we thought it should be.

Instead, you put us down. You pushed us aside. You made us feel "less than," worthless, and unworthy. But in the end, we have to thank you for this. You made us resilient. You made us determined. Your actions were our biggest motivators. You helped make us the people we are today, and we wouldn't change that for anything.

It's possible you weren't aware of what you were doing. Nevertheless, we hope you can learn as much from it as we did. In the future we hope you'll remember that we're all just people. In the future we hope you'll treat those who are different from you with respect and an open mind. This letter is to remind you to put yourself in the other's place before saying or doing something hurtful. I hope we can all be better for this experience, dear classmates.

Thank you again,

No Longer Invisible Us

I Could Hardly Understand One Sentence

Nada Kasim

After seven years I got used to living in a refugee camp, in Ethiopia, but then I had to move with my mom and six siblings to the United States. America is known for peace, equality, and freedom. It was also a place where I didn't understand the language, culture, and traditions. We didn't know anyone here. I'd never heard of Labor Day, Halloween, Thanksgiving, or Christmas. I could hardly understand one sentence when the teachers were explaining the lessons. I tried to improve my English by reading more books, watching more American movies, and making friends. Even though I'd studied English in the country I came from, people here speak in a totally different accent.

I Speak with an Accent

Nadifo Kasim

It is terrifying how speaking with an accent can change your path. Most of the time, when people don't like immigrants, it's not the ones who look and sound like them. It is fear of difference. It is judgment of intelligence. The truth is an accent is not a measure of intelligence. It is someone speaking your language using the rules of theirs.

A Conversation About School: Leftovers

Nadifo, Nada, Nimo, and Najma Kasim

Nimo: It is isolating being the only Somali girl in our classes. People don't talk to us, teachers don't call on us, and I think my classmates think we're dumb or something.

Nada: Yes! I may cover my head with a hijab, but it doesn't cover my brain. I can still think!

Nadifo: Often, a teacher asks a question and you know the answer, but you don't feel confident to answer because you feel like your classmates know better or they can say it better than you. So, you give up and assume that they should just answer. And then you feel like you don't know anything.

Nimo: Yes! And then when the teacher answers the question, you say, "Ohh I knew that!" That happens to me a lot.

Najma: I think teachers don't call on us because they think that's helpful. They don't want us to be embarrassed. But it is not really helpful.

Nada: Right. Why don't they try me and see what I can say?

Najma: They call on other foreign students. The teachers and the students talk to the exchange students. There was a girl from Switzerland. She knew every teacher and every student, and she had been in the school for only one year. And everybody knew her and everyone was saying "Hi!" to her.

Nada: Everyone got to talk to her and be like, "This is cool. You're from somewhere different."

Nimo: They'd say, "Tell us about Switzerland!"

Nada: There was a girl from Croatia in my history class, and whenever the teacher was talking about Europe she used to be so happy asking the student questions: "Hey you're from

Croatia. This is cool! Do you have this? Do you use this?" And then when she was talking about Somalia she wouldn't ask me anything.

Najma: My senior year, when I was taking that class, the teacher asked me a couple questions and I was thinking, "Ahh now you are getting it!" Some teachers try very hard.

Nimo: Everyone cares when you are from Europe. And when we say, "I come from Somalia," no one was ever like, "Oh how was it in Somalia?" They just ignore you. Every time, we are the leftovers. When we have to work with partners, we are always the leftovers. Sometimes they just ignore us. Some act like they didn't hear us, or they didn't understand us.

Nada: But when you feel that all the time, you just get used to it so much that you don't feel bad anymore. I like when I work by myself. Then I do better. I'm like, "yah, you don't need any of them."

Nimo: We get our work done sooner when we are by ourselves. We try harder than the others. I want to show them I can do better.

Najma: It's one of those things that can turn into a positive from a negative.

Nimo: But sometimes, you turn to your side and there is someone else who has been leftover as well. And then you become friends and you're not leftover at all.

Open Hearts

Bisharo Abdullahi

I'm from Djibouti. We moved to Green Bay on June 3rd, 2014. I started high school at Green Bay East and knew nothing! Four years later—to the day—I graduated, June 3rd, 2018.

When we first came to the United States, we lived in North Carolina. There was a Muslim community there, but there was not a lot going on. I thought it was boring. I thought, this is the United States I've heard about?

My first teachers in North Carolina were nice, though. They came to me with open hearts because I knew so little English. I was in this health class and I was failing. The teacher talked so fast! My resource support teacher had a beautiful heart and helped me. My grade went up and I ended up with a B!

A Conversation About School:
Not Like the Movies

Nadifo, Nada, Nimo, and Najma Kasim

Nadifo: We imagined it was going to be like in the movies!

Najma: Much more fun!

Nimo: I thought there would be a lot of people dancing!

Nadifo: Like in the movies!

Nimo: I thought it would be much harder like it was in Africa. But it was opposite. It was much easier than what I thought.

Nada: The teachers here are kind of nicer. You can't joke with the teachers back in Africa. You can't call them by their name. You just say "teacher."

Najma: It is a form of respect.

Nada: You know what was weird? Sitting next to boys. I remember in elementary school in Africa, there was a girls' class and a boys' class. It wasn't comfortable for us at first, sitting next to boys. But you get used to it.

Hi

Najma Kasim

In school, no one would talk to me. If one person said even "Hi," that person came closer than all the others. But there were still no real friends. Those who said hi to me, they meant a lot, even if they don't know.

$4 + 6(3) + 2$
$= 24 c^-$

$$:\overset{\cdot\cdot}{\underset{\cdot\cdot}{O}}:$$

$$\overset{\cdot\cdot}{\underset{\cdot\cdot}{O}} :: \overset{\cdot\cdot}{\underset{\cdot\cdot}{C}} :: \overset{\cdot\cdot}{\underset{\cdot\cdot}{O}}$$

$2Li_{(s)} + 2HCl_{(aq)} \rightarrow 2LiCl_{(s)} + H_{2(g)}$

→ $Li_{(g)}$ (Sublimation)

→ $HCl_{(aq)}$ (Bond energy) .... 166 KJ/mol

→ $Li^+ + e^-$ (ionization Energy) (427 KJ/mol) *2

$e^- \rightarrow Cl^{1-}$ (Electron Affinity) 520 KJ/mol

$Cl_{(g)} \rightarrow LiCl_{(s)} + H_{2(g)}$ (Lattice E) -349 KJ/mol

$H_{2(g)}$ (bon energy) -829 KJ/mol

.... +32 KJ/mol

→ $Li_{(g)}$ Sublimation

→ $Li^+_{(g)} + e^-$ Ioniz En (166 KJ/mol) * 2

→ $H_{(g)} + Cl^{1-}_{(g)}$ BE of HCl (520 KJ/mol) * 2

→ $H_{2(g)}$ BE of H_2 (427 KJ/mol) * 2

$e^- \rightarrow Cl^{1-}$ Elactron Af Cl (427 KJ/mol) * -1

$Cl_{(g)} \rightarrow LiCl_{(s)}$ LE (-349 KJ/

Plans

Where I'm From

Nasteho Kasim

I am from colorful curtains,
>From paintings on the wall
>and the mirrors in the corners of the house.

I am from the house in If Iyo Aakhiro, gray with yellow brick, rundown,
>It felt like warmth from the love of the family.

I am from the garden that the family planted,
>From Grandma's flowers,
>That kept the beauty of nature around the house.

I'm from *insha'Allah* at the end of a conversation
and eyebrows that curve,
>From Nimo and Najmo and Mubarak.

I'm from the family when they call you one time or two times but say
that they called more than a hundred times and
>From cooking big meals for the whole family on
> Saturdays and Sundays,
>From "Your first lie kills your next truth," something you were
>told as a child and
>"Don't open doors for strangers,"
>another thing you were told as a child.

I'm from the Quran.

I believe that Allah is the creator of all.

I'm from Somalia, near the Indian Ocean,

      From eating *halwo** and drinking tea with milk in the afternoons,
      From the time that my friends and I jumped over every stump
      on the road,

      And the time my aunt got my ears pierced
      and it didn't go as planned,

      From photo albums in the special bag that my mom keeps safe.

I am from walking on the warm sand barefoot, at home in my
legendary neighborhood.

---

* A sweet and spicy dessert

Hello Stranger

Maryam Husseyn

Hello stranger, I hope we get to know each other one day, not by talking behind my back, but really get to know each other, answering all your questions, all your thoughts about me, and solving all the misunderstanding. I know I am different, but I am also proud of who I am. You may try to hate me, maybe you were told bad things about me, but let me clarify these things for you.

I am a human and you are, too. I hope you were born from a loving family. So was I. I hope you were taught what's wrong and what's right. So was I. I hope you are free to wear what you want. So am I. I hope you practice whatever religion you think is right. So do I. I hope you dream of becoming who you want to be. So do I.

So tell me, stranger, how different do you think we are? Don't you think it hurts when you slander me, my family, my friends, my sisters, my neighbors, and our faith? Would you want to be hurt by a stranger? I would rather get to know you, and you me.

My dear stranger, I hope we get to know each other well. Please don't be confused by what you hear. I have come far from my home country, since the situation there forced us to leave. I really miss it. Wouldn't you miss your country too? Wouldn't you want someone to say, hello stranger?

Who Am I?

Nimco Sh. Abdullahi Hassan

My name is Nima Hassan and I was born and raised in a Somali refugee camp in Ethiopia. I went to school there, and I loved my childhood, regardless of the struggle of being a refugee. In the camp I had a neighborhood and a community.

Today, seven years after getting the chance to move to the United States, I attend a community college and I am heading to university to become a social worker. This is a big opportunity for me and I am grateful. Education is precious. I thank God every day for my having what millions of people are trying to cross oceans for. Everyone deserves a safe space to find out who they want to be— and learn to be it.

My Somali-American Dream

Zamzam Nur

I grew up in a decent house in the suburbs in America. Dakota County Community Development agency helped pay for our house. Both my parents worked low paying jobs, my mom at Sam's Club and my dad as a truck driver. We were doing okay when it was just my parents and my three siblings, but as the years went on our situation kept getting worse. My mom had two more kids and that destroyed our income. One day my parents fell apart. My dad bought us all one-way tickets to Somalia. He would stay behind to work and send us money.

They told us that we were going to Somalia to learn our language and culture, but we knew they didn't want to tell us the truth. They didn't want to break our hearts.

Life in Somalia was rough, but I'm glad we went because it would become the place where I gathered my aspirations. I realized that we were not the only ones struggling. My asthma became a problem while I was there, and I had to go to the hospital a lot. I saw a theme with every hospital I visited. They were all short staffed. It was such a problem that they would hire unqualified people and train them on a single task. The day I decided to become a doctor was the day my aunt died of something that could've been prevented if the doctors were properly trained and knew what they were doing. My aunt was taking a stroll when she tripped over a rock and fractured her leg. In the process of her surgery, they cut open one of her arteries and left it while they stitched her leg.

My dream of becoming an obstetrician-gynecologist stemmed from another incident that occurred during my stay in Somalia. I was visiting my sick uncle at a hospital and my mom and I passed by a room where a lady was giving birth. The midwife that was present was shouting for nurses to help her hold the lady's legs open. Since there were no nurses available, my mom and I stepped in. The whole situation was awry, from strangers helping to the way the midwife was handling the emerging baby, twisting it out and scratching its skin. My mom was screaming that she was killing the baby, but the midwife wouldn't listen. In the end, the baby's dead body emerged. My mother and I were shaken. I myself could not process it for weeks. I vowed that I would do everything in my power to make sure situations like that wouldn't happen under my watch.

In Somalia, I grew more in a matter of weeks than I had in years. We moved back to the United States, but my dream hasn't changed.

Moonlight

Nasteho Kasim

I sat next to the window in the corner of my empty room and the house felt deserted and foreign to me. I tried denying the truth, that we would move tomorrow and that I might never see this house again. This was the run-down house with yellow bricks, distinct from the neighboring houses. This was where I spent my childhood, running around with my sisters and brothers, playing rope and hopscotch in the backyard. This was where I lived, near my friends and close family, my uncles, my ayeeyo.

As I stood up to look at the enormous moon hovering in the sky, surrounded by his companions, the stars, I wondered, if the moon were alone, would it be able to shine? Would it feel lonely? My wondering was interrupted when my ayeeyo entered the room. She stood next to me as we watched the moon together and I felt my heart break with the thought of leaving her.

"Nasteho, what is wrong? Why are you crying?" She spoke tenderly, in her soft, soothing voice.

"Ayeeyo," I sobbed, "Why do we have to leave? I have you, my friends, and my school here and I don't want to go to another country."

She turned to me and hugged me and smiled. Ayeeyo told me how she hadn't been able to get an education beyond middle school and how lucky I was to be able to go to the United States. I would get a better education, an opportunity only fortunate people get. Then she told me something that changed my life forever.

She said, "Aqoon la'aan, waa iftiin la'aan" which translates "That without knowledge, there is no light."

From that moment, I decided to study hard and get the highest education I can get. I would live my life with new purpose, to finish school, to have a career that I choose for myself, to make my family and the people I care about proud.

I Want to Be a Lawyer

Najma Kasim

Education is the key to both my family and my future.

When I came to America, I was sixteen years old, but I didn't have the ability to ask for help, to understand and to be understood. It was like I was a child, learning how to talk. A child who had never heard about Halloween, Thanksgiving, Homecoming, Labor Day, or Christmas.

I have been waiting for so long to go to college. I want to be a lawyer because I hate to see people facing a dilemma without someone that can help. Somali newcomer immigrants who don't understand the language and the laws have a hard time understanding English-speaking lawyers and finding translators, but when I become a lawyer, I will help them because I don't need a translator to understand. I love the thought of helping out others because it makes me feel that I am a part of a much bigger world.

I Want to Be a Nurse

Bisharo Abdullahi

I'm going to be the second person in my family to graduate from high school. I want to make my parents proud—they work hard to give me a better education than they had. I'm going to college to become a registered nurse. I have always wanted to be a part of the medical field, that is my big dream, to give something back to my community. Nursing is the career version of my character and beliefs, of loving and caring for people who need it most.

I Want to Be a Doctor

Nadifo Kasim

My mom stopped school in seventh grade because of the civil war in Somalia. Which makes me the first generation of my family going to college. Education means a lot to me and to my family. I want to study science and math in college because these are my favorite subjects. I want to gain more knowledge. Education helps me understand the world around me and change it into something better. It helps me build opinions and have points of view on things in life. Once I have education no one can take it away and I can use it to help myself and others. I am very determined to keep learning. I want to be a doctor.

I Want to See Everything

Bisharo Abdullahi

In 2015, I thought, "I need to drive. You can't call someone every time you need a ride."

I told my brother, "Show me how to drive." (My sister is nicer than my brother, but I asked my brother.) I didn't understand anything with my brother. I went home and talked to my sister. She said, "I am very busy, but I can show you sometime." At that time, I was working at Tyson Foods and taking the bus to work. My sister was picking me up from work at night. She taught me to drive during that time, after work, at 11 o'clock at night! I was scared. But I learned how to drive.

I love remembering how much I've gone through and what I can do on my own. I want to travel and see the whole world someday. I want to see everything.

Through New Eyes

Yasmin Nur

Shock rocked through me as the ground underneath me shook. I didn't hear it, because of the headphones in my ears, but I knew it was a bomb. I took out my headphones and my family was shouting. Running outside, my five siblings and I saw a huge cloud of dust and smoke slowly creeping toward the sky, higher than the tallest buildings. I'd heard about things like this, but I didn't actually believe I would witness a bombing. I saw my siblings wide eyed, the younger ones laughing, not understanding. My mom was desperately clinging to her phone, trying to call every family member in the city. I closed my eyes, not wanting to picture the injured and dead.

I remember feeling trapped. I remember wanting to go back to Apple Valley, the suburb of Minneapolis where I used to live, and snuggle under my comforter. I was born in America. We were visiting Somalia to get to know my relatives and get closer to our religion, but for me, this was troubling. I lost twenty pounds in three months. I contracted malaria and became very ill.

Somalia did not have enough money, resources, or medical personnel to help the injured. In the days to come, many more of them joined the dead. Hearing about this lit a fire inside me. I despised those who had created the chaos and pain, but I began to appreciate the people around me. I started to say, more frequently, "How are you doing" and "Did you have a good day?" I cared more for my family and made an extra effort to show them that I loved them. I now know how easy it is for loved ones to be ripped away. I was only fourteen when I saw that bombing, but I knew then what I wanted to be: an emergency physician.

Although I had many hardships in Somalia, I also remember laughing a lot—playing with my siblings, swimming in the ocean, kicking soccer balls in the sand.

Especially Kids

Nadifo Kasim

I like to help people, especially kids. They give me hope for the future. I have over two hundred volunteer hours and most of them were helping children. I want my college major to relate to kids.

When I started school here, the teacher gave me homework. When I went home and tried to do it there were words that I could not understand. I had to translate them to my language. It was very hard because it was like teaching myself. There were times that I did not find the words in my language and had to use a dictionary or my mind to find out the meaning and complete the homework. Knowing three languages—Somali, Arabic, and English—helped me get through this challenge. I can use them to help others who speak these languages, especially people who are learning like I was, especially kids.

This Truth of Being Female

Nada Kasim

People tend to underestimate the capabilities of women. Even though the voices of women in today's society have become stronger, with more women entering offices traditionally held by men, women still are expected to place a high value on family roles and to commit themselves to homemaking and caregiving. There are still people in this world that judge people by their gender, no matter how hard women try to prove that they are capable of doing things men do. This truth of being female impacts my life a lot.

I Will Happily Help the Newcomers

Nimo Kasim

I can speak two languages and they are Somali and English. I will happily help the newcomers that have a hard time understanding English. For example, I can interpret in hospitals. More than anything, I would like to be a nurse!

There was a day in my geometry class, I failed a test. I asked my teacher if she could help me understand the material in order to retake the test. The second time, I got a perfect score. As well as learning geometry, I learned never give up.

I have lived in two continents, Africa and North America. Right now, everything is good.

Where We See Ourselves in Five Years:

Graduating from nursing school, traveling a lot.

I will be a social worker. I'll go to Africa and Asia.

I will stay here.

Studying to be a doctor—in a big city. I'll take my sisters with me.

I will be graduated from college with a degree in social work. I will have finished my memorization of the Quran and *insha'Allah* I will be married in two years.

In medical school, studying to be an emergency doctor, or an ear, nose, and throat doctor.

In medical school, studying to be an ob-gyn. I will practice in Minnesota before I move to Somalia. Then I want to open up my own medical school to reduce the high infant mortality rate in Somalia.

Mostly traveling—going back to visit my grandma and relatives, visiting people all over, not just in Somalia. My family is all around the world.

I will be a registered nurse and then I will go back to Somalia to help the little children and old people who need my help.

Having a passport, traveling anywhere.

I want to be a light for those who are facing hardship and darkness, like I did. I want to offer an ear to listen. I can't say exactly what I will be, but I will strive to continue my education and make a future for myself. This is especially important to my family, who have worked so hard to bring me here to the United States. My goal is to work hard every day so that I can put a smile on my mother's face, which is my ultimate happiness. I hope that I can help others in any way that will make their journey easier. I have many aspirations, but I know that the final plan belongs to God.

Epilogue

Now and Then

Nasteho Kasim

Mornings that begin by the Rooster
Eager to wake us from our slumbers,
Mesmerized by the changes in our lives.
Then
shelter, food, and (most important) water were scarce.
Now
is unexpected.
Love, rejoice, and reminisce.

A Note from Diana Delbecchi, ReSisters Co-Facilitator

The United ReSisters are a group of young Somali-American women working for peace and understanding in Green Bay, Wisconsin, and beyond. They named the group in honor of sisterhood and resistance: together they would use education, resilience, and love to stand up to hate, prejudice, and misunderstanding.

Meeting weekly since 2017, the group explored refugee and immigrant issues through the arts and work to build bridges in the community and confidence in themselves. They learn skills and map paths to higher education and reach out to others with visual art, literature, volunteering, and social events. At the time of this printing, theirs is the only group like this in Green Bay.

As facilitators of this group, my colleague Katherine Stockman and I try to remove, or at least offset, some of the obstacles these young women face. We provide guidance and connections so they may progress towards empowerment and achieve their dreams. Along the way, we have been honored and heartened by community support for the group. Local businesses, for example, seek to rent the ReSisters' inaugural mural painting, created as a tribute to the group members' Somali identity while telling the story of their path to Wisconsin. The mural is one way to engage the community in a conversation about diversity and inclusion, and already, these girls have a pivotal role in educating those ready to listen.

Twelve authors with twelve different stories to share: In making this book, the ReSisters have another opportunity to be cultural ambassadors and shapers of community conversation. I couldn't be prouder. What began as a book about their resettlement journeys blossomed into stories, poems, letters, and discussions of sisterhood, family, education, and paying tribute to those who helped along the way. Witness how the girls have grown and gained confidence through their long journeys to safety and relocation to our community. The ones whose story began here in the United States discovered themselves through an opposite journey that took them back to their cultural roots in Somalia, where they found out who they were meant to be. Together, the girls directed every stage of the project and made their own decisions about what to say and how to say it, resulting in a variety of writing styles, voices, and topics. Together, through the journey of writing, they decided which stories were important.

In the process of writing this book, our group saw many changes. Meeting weekly after school, we used our space to brainstorm book ideas, provide support to one another, and rejuvenate our spirits. In a matter of months, however, we celebrated half our members' graduation from high school and transition into college, honored the holy month of Ramadan and the feast of Eid, said goodbye to some of our sisters as their families relocated to another state, and lost our reliable meeting space in a community arts building where we had built a home for ourselves. The young authors' dedication to writing this book was the glue that kept us together. We took to meeting at coffee shops, libraries, my apartment, and even their homes—with the flexibility of locations, we spent the summer months meeting up to four times a week.

This book was a labor of love. Now, as its young authors offer the gift of their work to our community, I feel incredibly blessed to have witnessed its birth and helped tend to its transformation. The writings in these pages are testimonies of love, longing, and looking toward the future. They are expressions of deep gratitude and responsibility to our mothers, of heightened anxiety from a first day of school, of the aching wish to return to a time or place we once called home, and the excitement of blazing a new path.

I encourage you to listen—wholeheartedly—to these voices. They are extraordinary and ordinary, Somali and American and human; most important, they are the their own. Yet, they should sound familiar. No matter how different your own story may be, I hope you will recognize yourself in these words. I hope the humanity of each author's experiences will touch you. I'm quite sure they will surprise you, for these are not stereotypical, one-dimensional refugee stories of tragic pasts and limited futures. These girls are strong and facing forward. They are even stronger for being together. And what were the chances? Yes, they are all in some way from Somalia, but when you read about the many different paths that brought them to our community, to each other, to becoming the ReSisters, it feels like chance or, as I would like to believe, fate. I hope you will be as inspired by them as I continue to be.

I'm honored to have gotten to know these remarkable young women and to have worked with them on this project. The ReSisters are determined to build lives of purpose, giving back, and working towards peace. Will you join us?

A Note from Katie Stockman, ReSisters Co-Facilitator

In April of 2017, I joined Diana Delbecchi and Courtney Maye as a facilitator of the United ReSisters. We first met at an event centered on refugees at the Neville Museum in Green Bay. Diana had just returned from working at a camp for Syrian refugees in Greece and was speaking at a documentary that was part of the museum event and which I had brought my daughters to see. A couple weeks later, we met again at a small University of Wisconsin – Green Bay (UWGB) function aimed at familiarizing Somali students with higher education opportunities. There, I met some of the group members for the first time. Soon after, I started attending their weekly meetings, and never stopped.

Diana has her Master's in Human Rights. Courtney studied Social Justice and increasing equality and diversity through art. As a recent graduate of the UWGB Social Work Department (nearly) done with my Master's in School Social Work, my interests focus on the concepts of resiliency, growth mindset, cultural responsiveness, and protective factors for Somali youth. The three of us had our own goals for the group, with the overarching objective of supporting the girls. Diana focused on education, Courtney focused on art as a way to express themselves without needing (English) language, and my goal was to connect them to as many supports in as many different ways as I could within the community, to build up those protective factors and promote the extraordinary Somali culture throughout the Green Bay Area.

For example, COMSA (Community Services Agency of Northeast Wisconsin) hosted a hijabi party at the YWCA for Muslim and non-Muslim women and children to gather and bond and learn about each other through wearing beautiful head scarves and henna designs together. There was a hijabi shop in Green Bay at the time, and the Abdi sisters and their mother took me there before the party to pick out hijabs to bring for people who didn't have their own. They also showed me which henna to buy and took me to the Somali restaurant in town, to find more supplies and help me advertise for the event. My favorite part of such outings, by far, is the socializing. If you order food, you will end up drinking tea with whomever is sitting watching a soccer game. If there are women there, you will surely have a conversation about hijabs, fabric and how to pin it, and the latest fashions. You will hear about all of the shops in Minneapolis, and the ones they left behind in Africa. Then talk will turn to babies, and schooling, and marriages, and mothers. You will exchange phone numbers, take pictures, drink more tea, dress your children up in gorgeously colored scarves, and leave in a flurry of packages and hugs and "I will see you soon *insha'Allah* (God willing)," with a feeling of having just been adopted into a new family.

For another example, one of the young ladies had repeatedly expressed her interest in a career in social work and, more immediately, volunteering in the community. She and another group member came with me to a homeless shelter where I had previously interned and seen first-hand the need for female Somali interpreters. I was struck by the girls' natural empathy and capabilities in this context. So many people say to us, about the group, "we want to help," or, "you are so great to help them." What they do not understand is that these young women are competent, resilient, and strong. They have an intrinsic motivation to learn and to help others in their communities. They know it, too. They have agency. They are survivors, world travelers, who look for opportunities to help others, and the more they do the more I see their self-efficacy grow.

Another time, I drove seven of the ReSisters to hear Mariah Indrissi, famous for being the first hijab-wearing international model, speak. The girls were quiet during the Q&A, but after the presentation room emptied, they surrounded Ms. Indrissi and didn't stop talking, in Somali. I wished I knew what they were saying! I could tell from the hushed voices, bright smiles, arms around each other and hennaed fingers brushing away tears that it was important. I heard them laughing and agreeing over something to which they could all relate. I wished, with a flash of anger, that such special moments of connection and affirmation weren't so few and far between for them. I wished I could give them every day what Ms. Indrissi did that night. The drive home in my van was completely different from the drive there. The girls spoke in loud, confident Somali. Their experiences had been validated by a woman who has gone through similar struggles over the way she looks. They were happy and empowered.

There was the time some of the young women spoke to a local youth group at the Union Congregational United Church of Christ. These sweet, shy middle-schoolers raised their hands to ask questions about refugee resettlement and generally engage with the older newcomers. I was so proud of how gentle and kind the ladies were with the younger kids. This was cultural responsiveness in action: they took time, they respectfully answered questions, and in the end, it wasn't all about differences. It was about the love of math, being a middle child, and the excitement of the approaching summer months.

Then there was the time we went to *The Nutcracker*. The logistics of getting twelve Somali girls to the Meyer Theater in December are not easy. The tickets were donated, we had limited cars, limited parking, it was freezing, and they were dressed up like princesses. It was a matinee, we were running late, we lost tickets, we got tickets replaced, we couldn't all sit together... We finally got it all figured out, the lights blinked signaling that the show was going to begin, we started to split up to find our seats when suddenly all of their cell phone alarms went off. It was the Call to Prayer. Courtney, my mom, who was helping out, and I told the ticket takers that the girls needed a place to pray, immediately. Without missing a beat, they led us to a small, beautifully decorated and curtained-off room. The girls removed their shoes, found the East, and began to pray. The lights stopped blinking. The ticket takers bowed their heads. The entire theater was silent, and latecomers stopped to bow their heads as well. That curtain held for twelve praying girls. The music waited. When they were done, they gracefully entered the balcony where people gave up their seats so they could all sit together with first-row views. Nasteho wore diamonds as a crown and the entire day was magical.

I taught some of them how to drive and helped them get their licenses. As more than one of them note in this book, driving is empowering, especially in Green Bay. It is also a special skill in Green Bay for several months of the year, when snow and ice add extra challenges. But, mostly, the young women teach me—about journeys, family, friendship, and faith; resilience, courage, and grace. And sisterhood. I am deeply and forever grateful for all our times together.

Acknowledgments

It took more than a village to make this book: it took the town of Green Bay and beyond. We are deeply grateful to the following people and organizations.

Julie Ollmann, librarian at East High School, for first introducing us to these remarkable young women and being supportive of the founding of this group.

The ARTGarage for the beautiful space that allowed for many memories to be made.

Courtney Maye, Artist Extraordinaire and social justice advocate without whom this group would cease to exist! Her artistic talent and love created a safe and brave space for them to paint and (re)design their lives.

Marina Delbecchi, Luul Abdi, and Angie Flannigan for their friendship, sisterhood, and constant support in enrichment programming and experiences.

The educational institutions of University of Wisconsin - Green Bay (UWGB), St. Norbert College, Northeast Wisconsin Technical College, and Green Bay Area Public Schools for welcoming and championing the ReSisters.

Dr. Katia Levintova for her support from the UWGB Political Science Department and approving formal internships through the ReSisters.

Dr. David Coury and Dr. Jon Shelton for increasing access to the University for the Somali community, and specifically advocating for the group to focus on higher education.

Dr. Robert Pyne from the Norman Miller Center for Peace, Justice and Public Understanding and Amy Kundinger from College Advancement at St. Norbert College.

Dr. Cristina Ortiz and Dr. Mary Jacobi for being powerful, educated women and for coming to speak to the group about college transitions and offering their mentorship.

The UWGB Social Work Department for providing inspiration to be social advocates and agents of change.

COMSA, specifically Sheik Hassan, Mahamad Mahamed Raage, and Said Hassan who have always rallied for and with the ReSisters. Support from these giants in the local Somali community has allowed for collaborative events and partnerships.

The Neville Museum for commissioning and displaying the first Somali artwork for their *Our Brown County* exhibit.

Pastor Bridget Flad at Union Congregational United Church of Christ for her invitation and warm welcome when the ReSisters came to speak to the youth groups.

Celestine Jeffries and the Mayoral Celebration Fund for funding the leadership training at JOSHUA.

Kate Lemieux Espinosa for her efforts and for coordinating the (one and only) mural rental at Humana.

Trina Lambert, Emilie Heil, and Rachel Burger from Aldo Leopold Community School, who welcomed the group for Exploratory Week and Aldo Legacy Days.

Jacob Higbee, Lyle Keeble, and Xavier Horkman from JAX of All Ideas Media for their beautiful and honest depiction in the documentary they created about the ReSisters, jaxofallideas.com.

Jen Jones from Admissions and Gail Sims-Aubert from Residential Housing at the UWGB for collaborating to make it possible for four of our ReSisters to live together on campus for their first year of college.

Green Bay Catholic Diocese for awarding the group the Rice Bowl Grant which funded laptop purchases for the members.

Support of Urban Projects grant program for awarding the group its first funding that allowed for many art projects to continue.

Mickey Mikeworth of Project Elf, who decorated the Kasim sisters' first house in the United States and literally made them feel at home.

TitleTown Publishers for signing on from the beginning.

Stephanie Higgs and Elizabeth Paulson of Two Shrews Press for taking us on and believing in the powerful stories of these young women.

Ifrah Mansour, Bahame Tom Nyanduga, and Michelle Langenfeld for their powerful forewords.

Libby Clarke for making this book something beautiful to behold.

Kara Counard of Bloom Photography by Kara for capturing incredible images and helping to document a beautiful moment in time for these young ReSisters.

Our gratitude also to The Mauthe Center, The North East Wisconsin Dance Organization, and the Women's Fund of Greater Green Bay.

Finally, a special thanks to our families: Jeff, Mimi, Lola, and Walter Daffner; and Kristal, Mia, Marina, and Marco Delbecchi, all of whom embraced the group with admiration and respect.

Glossary

abaya	a black dress that comes in a variety of styles
aabo	dad
Allah	God
al-Shabaab	a terrorist organization in Somalia
alhamdulillah	"Praise Allah"
anjero	food similar to sourdough crepes
Aw-Barre	a refugee camp in Ethiopia
ayeeyo	grandma
baati	a Somali dress with a long, fluid, wide-sleeved silhouette
baba	dad
beer iyo basa	camel or goat liver and onions
dugsi	Islamic school where younger children learn manners and older children learn the Quran
Eid (al-Fitr)	the major Muslim holiday at the end of Ramadan; literally "festival of breaking the fast"
Eid (al-Adha)	the second Eid of the year, literally "festival of the sacrifice"; this is when Muslims make their pilgrimage to Mecca.
famix	a supplementary food ration for young children and pregnant and lactating mothers.
habo	aunt
Hajj	the pilgrimage of Muslims to Mecca, in Saudi Arabia, that teaches lessons of unity, sacrifice, and brother and- sisterhood. For Muslims, the Hajj is the fifth and final pillar of Islam.
halwo	a sweet dessert

hijab	a head covering
hooyo	mom
If Iyo Aakhiro	a zone in the Aw-Barre refugee camp, in Ethiopia. The name translates "the light in the afterlife."
imam	Islamic priest and scholar
insha'Allah	"God willing"
jihad	the spiritual struggle within oneself
Kaaba	The cube-shaped building in Mecca that is the most sacred Muslim pilgrim shrine. Inside the Kaaba is the black stone believed to have been given by Gabriel to Abraham. Muslims everywhere, every day pray facing the direction of the Kaaba.
kitab	book
masjid	the mosque
Muhammad	Muhammad is the last and final messenger, peace be upon him.
nasheed	an Islamic saying or Islamic song without music
qabil	tribe—can be positive cultural identity or divisive, antagonistic stance against other tribes
Quran	the holy book of Islam
Ramadan	the ninth month of the Islamic calendar, the month that the Quran was revealed to the prophet Muhammad. During Ramadan, Muslims around the world fast from sunrise to sunset.
sambusa	a type of stuffed pastry or bread in a triangular shape
uunsi	A type of incense rock, made of incense combined with white copper and sugar.

Resources

"What If Aid Agencies Were Among the Most Powerful Forces on Earth?" The British writer Caitlin Moran posed this question in a series of essays on the global migration crisis.* What if, she muses, "aid agencies suddenly had as much political and financial leverage as arms dealers and chemical weapons manufacturers"? Imagine. (As the British songwriter John Lennon once sang.)

Aid agencies are not, currently, among the most powerful forces on earth, but they are as powerful as the people who support them. What can you do? Here are some of our favorites, if you would like to give your support.

Casa Alba Melanie – Helps newly-arrived immigrants in Green Bay. *www.asaalba.org*

Community Services Agency of Northeast Wisconsin (COMSA) – Specializes in the history and needs of the Somali immigrant community. *www.comsausa.org*

Emily's List – Supports pro-choice Democratic women—like Somali-American Congresswoman Ilhan Omar—for office. *www.emilyslist.org*

International Refugee Assistance Project (IRAP) – Legal advocacy for refugees and displaced people. *www.refugeerights.org*

Literacy Green Bay – One local example of how invaluable literacy organizations are to newly resettled immigrants and refugees. *www.literacygreenbay.org*

Preemptive Love Coalition – Works abroad, on the ground, to help families fleeing violence. *www.preemptivelove.org*

Project Elf Minneapolis – Provides home furnishings and long-term support to people getting out of poverty. *www.projectelfmn.com*

---

* Moran, Caitlin, *Moranifesto.* (New York, Harper Perennial, 2016). 224-235.

Sharing & Caring Hands – In Minneapolis, including the Mary's Place of Nadifo Kasim's story "Adapting."
www.sharingandcaringhands.org

Somali Youth and Family Development Center – Another excellent effort in Minneapolis to help Somali families thrive in their new community.
www.somfam.org

United Nations Human Rights Office of the High Commissioner.
www.ohchr.org

Women's Fund – A local Green Bay organization that promotes community programs that empower women and inspire girls.
www.womensfundgb.org

World Relief – Locally World Relief Fox Valley, this organization sponsors newcomers from all over Africa, Asia, and the Middle East.
www.worldrelief.org

About the Authors

Bisharo Abdullahi, at five feet three inches, is small but mighty! Bisharo is always first to show up, always positive and enthusiastic. She is a huge fan of glam, so it's Bisharo we look to for the most fabulous shoes and big, bright smile. She doesn't have her own siblings in the group, but she is a sister to all. Her motivation to get to group meetings, even in the blustery Green Bay snow, shows her commitment to the mission of the ReSisters. Newcomers to the meetings and in the community always feel they have an immediate friend with Bisharo.

Nima Hassan has displayed a love for social justice since we met her. Her conversations revolve around equality, human rights, and devotion to her religion. Her perspective and voice encourage other women to express their values openly, she often invites new women to the group, and she serves as an advocate for her colleagues at Walmart. Nima looks for every opportunity to learn, advocate, and share resources. She plans to become a social worker, and we know she will be an asset to any community. In summer of 2018 her family moved to Minnesota and the group has missed her presence dearly.

Najma Hussein is endearingly referred to as "baby Najma," primarily as a joke, because she is often the most mature member of the group. She serves the mosque each week by teaching the Quran to children and hopes to one day assume a profession that will allow her to give back. She is the most recently resettled in our group and lived in Ethiopia without her parents before arriving to the United States. Her kind heart and commitment to her faith shine through her poems and stories as she details her journey to be reunited with her mother after almost a decade apart.

Hafsa and **Maryam Husseyn**, sisters a couple years apart, are often mistaken for twins. They share a lightheartedness that is contagious. The Husseyn sisters arrived in the United States in 2014 and spent four and a half years in Green Bay. After a devastating loss, the family decided to start fresh in Minnesota.

With her vintage aviator glasses, **Hafsa** exudes cool. She is spunky, theatrical and, lucky for us, the friendliest kind of cool. She keeps all of us laughing with her quick wit and fun-loving dance moves. Upon meeting her, you wouldn't know how much she has had to overcome, but her writing gives an honest and vulnerable look into her time growing up fleeing war and conflict.

Maryam is the younger sister, with maturity and poise that belie her age. Her deep compassion for others led her to obtain her CNA certification and work at a local nursing home while she completed classes at the technical college, earning an income for her family during a time when they needed it most. But Maryam is not all seriousness: turn on some Bollywood music and her irresistible smile invites everyone around her to let loose and have fun.

Nimo, Najma, Nadifo, Nade (Nada), and **Nasteho Kasim** lived in a refugee camp in Ethiopia with their mom, two brothers, grandma, three uncles, and a great-grandma. The five sisters arrived in the United States with their mother in 2014 and waited twelve years to be reunited with their father, in the fall of 2018.

Gracious and humble is **Nimo**. She has a way of making all feel welcome with her sparkly, warm eyes, and her inviting hugs—a way of turning outsiders into lifelong friends. Nimo is small, but she is powerful, challenging anyone who would dismiss her or her sisters. She is quick to offer encouraging words and helpful advice to others, and her judgment is often sought. Her nurturing presence encourages her siblings and will help her become an excellent nurse.

Sweet, sweet, **Najma** steals everyone's heart! She has a quick mind, but chooses her words carefully, which is why we jumped for joy when she showed interest in law. Najma might first appear shy, but she is articulate, empathetic, and an advocate for what is good in the world. She gives all of herself to her siblings and is devoted to her loved ones. It is hard to believe her sisters' laughing tales of her running away in defiance from any adult that asked her to sit nicely.

Nadifo is a quiet observer, happy to go with the flow of her sisters. She is patient and attentive to others, and the constant companionship of her sisters has gifted her with an intuition that perfectly aligns with her role as a caregiver—to those around her and when she becomes the doctor she plans to be. She is a straight-shooter, a talented artist, and good at everything she tries.

Nada never pretends to like something she doesn't, always shares her mind, and has high standards for herself and those around her. Her dedication to perfection is palpable. She edited and re-edited stories and poems over and over. She constantly amazes us with new passions and talents, like when she taught herself how to sew from YouTube videos, when she couldn't find clothing in town that fit her style. Nada is her real name, but it was misspelled "Nade" by immigration officials.

Nasteho is bubbly with a heart of gold. She is a natural observer of the human spirit, always tuned into what those around her are feeling. She makes everyone feel comfortable and welcome, while always keeping us laughing. Her eternal optimism steered her writing toward her devotion to religion and sharing her favorite things. She was still a very young child while living in the camps of Ethiopia and does not remember her home in Somalia. Now she is a powerful voice in the group and effortlessly leads others.

Yasmin and **Zamzam Nur** were born in the United States to parents who, after fleeing Somalia in the 1990s, met and fell in love stateside. The Nur sisters are both dedicated scholars, both striving to work in the medical field.

Yasmin graduated from high school in 2018 and now attends the University of Wisconsin – Green Bay full time. Her natural leadership ability has already propelled her into a prominent role in student government, where she represents students from the Multi-Ethnic Student Affairs office. She didn't stop there! She also founded the Somali Student Union and has had a positive influence on her peers. Her power and presence will continue to serve her well as she pursues her passion for medicine with a laser focus.

Zamzam is a senior in high school, a rising star recently accepted into the University of Wisconsin – Madison. She has a heart of gold, working diligently throughout high school to become involved in groups such as Health Occupation Students of America and Future Business Leaders of America. Her dream of returning to Somalia to work as an ob-gyn is not far from reach; her spirit of goodwill carries her forward.